From Writing to Composing

An Introductory Composition Course

Beverly Ingram
Carol King

TEACHER'S MANUAL

Second Edition

CAMBRIDGE UNIVERSITY PRESS
Cambridge, New York, Melbourne, Madrid, Cape Town,
Singapore, São Paulo, Delhi, Mexico City

Cambridge University Press
The Edinburgh Building, Cambridge CB2 8RU, UK

Published in the United States of America by Cambridge University Press, New York

www.cambridge.org
Information on this title: www.cambridge.org/9780521671361

First published 2005

A catalogue record for this publication is available from the British Library

ISBN 978-0-521-67136-1 Paperback

Table of Contents

Introduction

What is a good way to get ready to teach with *From Writing to Composing*?

For maximum benefit, read the To the Teacher pages that open the Student Book (SB), along with these two introductory pages. The material here is meant to supplement, not replace, that more comprehensive introduction.

What is the underlying relationship between the instructional activities in *From Writing to Composing*?

The flowchart in Figure 1 shows how the streams of instruction in the text are interrelated. One major stream is *writing,* which consists of practice activities that provide work with useful vocabulary, content, and organizational patterns students will need later in composing activities. The other major stream is *composing,* which builds upon the writing activities but allows students to use their own experiences and expertise in the creation of multi-draft compositions.

As shown in Figure 1, the products of both streams of instruction are equally important at this proficiency level, and each is honored in a special project. The portfolio project collects all the *writing* practice, and the publication project shares the final, polished compositions that students have *composed.*

Figure 1

listening and speaking

	Writing	Composing
1st person "I" writing	Writing practice *Narratives, Letters & e-mail, Reflective writing, and so on*	Multi-draft composing *Real-life stories, Field trips, Daily routines, and so on*
3rd person Formal style Expository	Writing practice *Organization patterns, such as enumeration, chronology, classification*	Multi-draft composing *Personal expertise, Ways of Doing X, Types of Y, Armchair tours*
	Portfolio project *Guided Independent*	Publication project

listening and speaking

Furthermore, as shown in Figure 1, *From Writing to Composing* teaches both first-person style, used for narration, letters and e-mails, and reflective writing; and third-person style, used for more formal, expository, academic writing. Both styles are important, so each is practiced in the writing stream and applied in the composing stream.

Finally, as Figure 1 indicates, we find that all students at this proficiency level need a great deal of listening and speaking experience. They need to participate in listening-speaking activities on each topic before trying to write about it. They need the support of oral interaction at points during the writing process, and they benefit from the reinforcement and closure provided by listening and speaking after writing. In short, we envision that all writing and composing ventures will be embedded in a communicative classroom

How can I help my students keep track of their portfolio assignments?

We have found the Table of Contents (TOC) page shown in Figure 2 to be very useful. We use it as the first page in our students' portfolio folders where they collect their writing practice assignments.

When a portfolio assignment is made, students can write its title and its number on their TOC list, along with the designation IPWA or GPWA, as appropriate. Then, they can number each assignment in the upper right hand corner of the page as they put it in their portfolio.

This simple system serves as an ongoing reminder of what needs to be done and is remarkably effective in giving students motivation to complete all of the writing practice assignments.

Figure 2

Name: ____________________

Class: ______________ **Portfolio Project** Semester/Term: ________

Guided-Practice Writing Assignments (GPWA)	**Independent-Practice Writing Assignments (IPWA)**
• The book or teacher will give you some or all of the words or sentences. • Focus on accuracy. • Use good format.	• Spend about 15–30 minutes writing. • Write 100–200 words. • Focus on communicating ideas and writing efficiently. • Don't worry much about mistakes. • Use good format.

Table of Contents

1. Letter about myself	*Activity 1.4 (p. 6)*	*GPWA*
2. An important person	*Activity 2.2 (p. 10)*	*IPWA*

Part One

Getting Started

Unit 1 Dear Classmates

Unit 1 uses familiar, concrete genres with clear audience and purpose to help everyone in the class get acquainted and start building a sense of community.

1.1 Letters and e-mail, page 2

To introduce this activity and focus everyone's attention, tell the class that you are going to do a five-second observation test. Give students five seconds to look at page 2. Then, have them close their books, and while using one hand to hold the place, have students answer questions that are the same as or similar to the following.

What did you see?
Did you see a letter?
Did you see two letters?
What else did you see?
Did you see an e-mail message?
Did you see two e-mail messages?
Did you see any names?
What is a name that you saw?
Did you notice any words?
What is a word that you remember?
Did you see any questions?
How many questions?
Do you want to look at the page again?

Give the class five more seconds to look at the page. Then, have students look up and ask them some or all of the same questions again. After that, start the pair work with the questions given in the book.

1.2 A letter about a classmate, pages 3–4

In Activity A, if you have an odd number of students, you can do the interview with the remaining student while keeping an eye on the progress of the rest of the class.

In Activity B, the letter is designed to look easy and nonthreatening. Yet, as students write it, you can get useful information about their readiness and confidence as writers in English. (If you want an additional, less-guided writing sample, have students look at the pictures on page 26 and try writing the story as best they can.) The letter includes the number of people in the class, so review the spelling of numbers from zero to one hundred. While the rules about expressing numbers vary widely depending on the context (e.g., newspapers vs. books vs. scientific or statistical writing), here are some fairly standard rules. 1) Spell out a number if you can write it in one word or two unhyphenated words. If not, use numerals. 2) If a number is the first word in a sentence, always write it out. 3) Use numerals with units of measurement (e.g., 3 meters).

1.3 Features of a letter, page 5

The file card in this activity is the first of 23 file cards that present key concepts throughout the book. A complete list of the file cards with their page numbers appears on page ix of the *To the Teacher* pages in the Student Book (SB). You can either emphasize the information on the cards or not depending on the needs of your students and course goals.

Note that the format of this letter is a semi-block style. Another popular format, especially for business letters, is the block style in which all parts are aligned at the left margin, and paragraphs are set apart by double line spacing, not indentation.

1.4 More letters, page 6

This is a great place for teachers to join in! We have had good results from adding a letter about ourselves to this activity. As class work or homework, have students read the letter that you have written about yourself, and ask them to write two or three questions to get more information about you. Then, answer their questions orally, or write answers to some of them in the e-mail exchange activity that ends the unit.

If possible, tape the letters to the class onto the classroom walls, and have students circulate and read them as if in a gallery, as shown in the picture on page 35 in the SB. Make a handout with a content question about each letter for students to write answers to as they read.

1.5 E-mail messages, page 6

This activity establishes e-mail as a means of communication outside of class. You can use it constructively throughout the course. This is also another great place for teachers to join in. Via e-mail, answer some of the questions about you that students wrote in Activity 1.4. Alternatively, if you did not write a letter about yourself in Activity 1.4, you can send an e-mail now instead.

A Possible answers, page 6:

2 At the top, these e-mail messages have four additional parts – the *From* line, the *To* line, the *Cc* line, and the *Subject* line. The date is labeled and is in a different position. The paragraphs are not indented. The closing is against the left margin. There is no handwritten signature.

Unit 2 Friends and Relatives

Unit 2 introduces the portfolio project, capitalization and punctuation, and simple sentences. This unit encourages students to use computers if possible.

2.1 Important people, page 9

Have students write their own name in the center circle of the diagram. Discuss the word *diagram.* Focus on the three content words in the diagram, eliciting examples of each category given. Then, brainstorm for other categories that are useful in their lives. After students write specific names in each circle, have them work with a partner, asking and answering the written questions as a warm-up for Activity 2.2.

2.2 Independent-practice writing, page 10

This is the first of a series of 13 independent-practice writing assignments, one per unit after Unit 1. Activity 2.2 provides questions for students to discuss with a partner before beginning to write. You can use each independent-practice assignment once or several times because each contains several suggested topics. Be sure students understand that their focus should be on fluency not accuracy, on communicating ideas not practicing grammar. Also, emphasize how many minutes they have to write. This time, have students handwrite or use the computer lab during class time and count their words after finishing. (Computer programs have useful tools that students can use to count words.) Subsequent independent-practice assignments can be done as timed-writing practices in class or assigned as computer lab work or as homework. These papers will go into the portfolios that students start in Activity 2.3.

2.3 The portfolio project, pages 10–11

Before class, read pages viii and 146–8 (Appendix 3) in the SB. Before beginning Activity A, discuss the word *soccer* with the class. To develop students' listening skills, you can have students close their books and listen while you read the statements aloud.

For Activity B, if possible, show actual samples of the type of folder that your students will use for collecting their writing practice. Sometimes the school or teacher will provide a folder for each student, and sometimes the students will need to buy and bring to school a suitable folder. (We have found simple folders available in the United States for 5 to 10 cents each during August back-to-school sales, and we stock up then on folders to give students during the year.) Make sure students understand the meaning of the words *folder* (physical object) and *portfolio* (collection of a person's work).

Have students write their names on the cover of the folder, in the top right corner, for easy distribution. Ask students to personalize or decorate the covers of their folders or to make a personal title page to insert in the new folder. If possible, provide colored markers or pencils. This activity will showcase the work of students whose talents may be more artistic than linguistic and give them the chance to experience success and recognition in your class early in the course.

2.4 *Introduction to capitalization and punctuation,* pages 11–12

Activity A can be fun. The missing components are capital letters and two end punctuation marks, specifically the question mark and period. Let students try to figure out the number of sentences on their own but provide as much help as needed. Emphasize the point that the paragraph is hard to read because of the missing components. Ask students if they know how to show the beginning (with a capital letter) and the end (with end punctuation) of a sentence. The file card in Activity B presents the information needed to correctly rewrite the paragraph.

B Answer, page 12:

> The Portfolio Project
>
> Do you already have a collection of your writing? Many people do. They keep diaries and journals during their life. They want to write down their ideas and save their writing. The portfolio project will help you save your writing from your writing course.

2.5 *Introduction to sentences,* pages 12–14

Put the sentences from the Activity A file card on the blackboard or overhead but omit the capitals and punctuation. Ask students to help you add these elements. Then, ask students to find the verb and then the subject in each example. The subject-verb combination is the key to correct sentence structure. The paragraphs on page 13 have correct sentence structure, capitalization, and punctuation. The paragraph in Activity A2 has only simple sentences although one of them has compound verbs (#5) and another has compound subjects (#6). The paragraph in Activity B1 also has a simple sentence with compound verbs (#5), a simple sentence with compound subjects (#7), a compound sentence (#4) and a complex sentence (#6). You can emphasize these or not, depending on the needs of your students and your course goals.

A Answers, page 13:

1 ten
2 sentence #5
3 sentence #6
4 The subject comes after the verb, not before it.

B Answers, page 13:

> My Dog Shorty
>
> At home in Mexico, I have a little dog. She is an important part of our family. We call her Shorty. She is a little fat, but her shape is very cute. All my friends know her name and play with her. My father sometimes gets angry with her because she eats plants in his garden. His tomatoes and flowers are her favorite snacks. I would like to pet Shorty right now.

Activity C reviews the topics of important people and staying in touch. Have students put their finished work in their new portfolios for you to check at the end of the week.

C Answer, page 14:

My Twin Brothers

Today I want to write about my two really wonderful older brothers. They are twins and were born on Christmas Eve. They are university students in Japan. One brother goes to a university in Osaka, and the other goes to a university in Kyoto. Therefore, they do not live at home with my family right now. They are majoring in geography. This year they will graduate from their universities and are thinking about graduate school. We usually stay in touch by e-mail, but I sent them a beautiful postcard last week. I miss them very much and want to see them soon.

You can use Activity D as an opportunity to have students apply what they have learned about capitalization, punctuation, and sentence structure to their own writing. This activity also allows students, for the first time, to use their portfolios to reread and revise their own work.

Unit 3 Staying in Touch

Unit 3 introduces 1) dictation, a key activity; 2) basic paragraph structure; and 3) the format for both handwritten and typed student papers. It also continues the portfolio project begun in Unit 2.

3.1 Enumeration dictation, pages 15–18

This is the first of five multipurpose dictation sequences in the book, each of which will give students integrated practice in writing while listening, reinforce correct sound-symbol relationships, and improve attention to spelling and punctuation. Furthermore, as used in this book, the dictations give students experience with variations in sentence structure, present aspects of paragraph organization, promote interaction by introducing new vocabulary and ideas for discussion, and serve as springboards for students' own basic formal paragraphs.

The following lists some points to bear in mind when working with any of the dictation sequences in the book. In each dictation sequence, students write from dictation three times. A pencil icon marks each of these three dictation exercises.

- When giving the paragraph dictations, follow the instructions in the SB in the box at the top of page 142 in Appendix 2. If possible, make an audio recording of the dictations to use in class to discourage requests for repetition and to give students practice with recorded materials. If a friend or colleague is willing to record for you, your students can get experience with another voice.
- In the first dictation, called *Dictation, Version 1,* students write the dictation paragraph as best they can without having heard it before. This exercise stimulates interest in the paragraph because it is the answer to the puzzle students are trying to solve as they attempt to write what they hear. After checking this initial paragraph, students talk about its content, analyze its structure, and add supporting information.
- In the second dictation exercise, called *Self-correcting dictation,* students practice writing new sentences that use vocabulary from both the first dictation paragraph and the supporting information.
- The third dictation, called *Dictation, Version 2,* is a dictation quiz in which students write a paragraph that is a reconfiguration of the original paragraph and some supporting information.

To start Activity A, generate interest, and focus attention, tell the class that you are going to do a five-second observation test. Give students five seconds to look carefully at the photo on page 15. Then, have them close their books, and while using one hand to hold the place, have students answer questions that are the same as or similar to the following.

Was there a man or a woman in the photo?
Was the woman old or young?
Was the woman listening and writing?
What do you think she was writing?
Was she using a computer or a phone?
Was she using a cell phone or a regular phone (land line)?
Was she writing on a pad or in a spiral notebook?
Was she writing on a small pad or a large one?
Was her hair long or short?

Was she wearing a T-shirt or a blouse?
Was the blouse white?
Did the blouse have long sleeves or short sleeves?
Was she writing with her right hand or her left?
Were there circles or squares in the background?

If needed, give students five more seconds to study the photo and continue the practice by repeating some or all of the questions. After that, do steps A1 and A2, given in the book.

A Possible answers, page 15:

taking a phone message; taking notes in a class, a presentation, or a meeting; writing down directions to someone's house for a party; writing down a phone number, Web address, and/or interesting information that you hear on TV or the radio

2 Dictation helps you develop your ability to write things down quickly and accurately and to improve your spelling and punctuation. Thus, it helps you prepare for notetaking in classes and meetings by giving you practice in writing while you are listening. In addition, dictation helps you see how native speakers group words into phrases and link words when they speak. Words are separate on a page but sound connected when people speak.

Activity C makes a reference to the Mini-Handbook. Before using the Mini-Handbook, read about it at the bottom of page ix in the SB.

C Answers, page 16:

4 **a** relatives **b** communicate **c** ways **d** e-mail **e** phone

Activity D introduces the term and concept, *enumeration.* Some teachers and texts use the term *listing* instead, so you may want to emphasize both words. We have found that adult beginners often get considerable satisfaction from learning the occasional long and difficult word, so we deliberately chose *enumeration.*

In Activity E, students practice a very important skill by adding support to the original dictation paragraph. As in later dictation-based units, the paragraph produced in this activity will serve as a starting point for students' own paragraph compositions.

E Answer, page 17:

Staying in Touch

People today have three good ways of staying in touch with friends and relatives. The first way is writing letters. People love getting personal letters. The second way is making phone calls. Telephoning is fast, and cell phones are making some long-distance calls more economical. The third way is sending e-mail messages. This electronic method is both quick and convenient. Therefore, there is really no technological reason for people not to communicate.

(72 words)

The Activity E paragraph has, clearly, very little support. In fact, it contains the barest minimum. Whenever your students are capable, whether now or later in the course, you should guide them to develop the paragraph further by adding more sentences of support based on examples and facts from their personal lives. The following is an example of the type of work you should elicit. You may copy this paragraph and share it with your students if you wish.

Staying in Touch

People today have three good ways of staying in touch with friends and relatives. The first way is writing letters. People love getting personal letters. For example, I jump with joy over letters from my host family in Costa Rica. I read the letters several times and keep them in a special place. The second way is making phone calls. Telephoning is fast, and cell phones are making some long-distance calls more economical. For instance, my roommate Kim talks to her brother in Miami every day because she has lots of free long-distance minutes. The third way is sending e-mail messages. This electronic method is both quick and convenient. Many times, international students, including me, prefer e-mail because it is faster and easier than writing letters. It is also cheaper than making international calls. Therefore, there is really no technological reason for modern people not to communicate because they have three good ways of staying in touch.

 (157 words)

In Activity E, when students have finished adding supporting information from their personal experiences, either you or some willing students can reformat some well-developed paragraphs as cloze exercises that can be used in later classes. Use one of the best individual paragraphs or a composite for this activity. Type or handwrite (or have a student or students type or handwrite) the paragraph in a cloze-exercise format by substituting a blank line for every sixth or seventh word. Make copies of the cloze exercise for all of the students, who must fill the blanks with logical words (reading cloze) or fill them with the words they hear as the paragraph is read aloud (listening cloze). If you do a listening cloze, you can either read the story or make a cassette recording for whole-class or small-group listening.

If you have your students write out or type the cloze exercise for the whole class, they have extra incentive to produce neat, legible, correct papers. On the other hand, if you do the writing or typing, you can correct anything in the paper that might still be incorrect or incomprehensible to student readers. This is particularly useful in giving closure to a composition sequence when you have not had enough time for students to revise and edit to achieve a polished final product.

On the next page, you will see a cloze version of a well-developed paragraph. You are welcome to photocopy this cloze exercise (and other cloze exercises that appear later in this Teacher's Manual).

Staying in Touch

People today have three good ______(1) of staying in touch with ______(2) and relatives. The first way ______(3) writing letters. People love getting ______(4) letters. For example, I jump ______(5) joy over letters from my ______(6) family in Costa Rica. I ______(7) the letters several times and ______(8) them in a special place. ______(9) second way is making phone ______(10). Telephoning is fast, and cell ______(11) are making some long-distance ______(12) more economical. For instance, my ______(13) Kim talks to her brother ______(14) Miami every day because she ______(15) lots of free long-distance ______(16). The third way is sending ______(17) messages. This electronic method is ______(18) quick and convenient. Many times, ______(19) students, including me, prefer e-mail ______(20) it is faster and easier ______(21) writing letters. It is also ______(22) than making international calls. Therefore, ______(23) is really no technological ______(24) for modern people not to ______(25) because they have three good ______(26) of staying in touch.

 (159 words)

Possible cloze test answers: **1** ways; **2** friends; **3** is; **4** personal; **5** with; **6** host; **7** read; **8** keep; **9** The; **10** calls; **11** phones; **12** calls; **13** roommate; **14** in; **15** has; **16** minutes; **17** e-mail; **18** both; **19** international; **20** because; **21** than; **22** cheaper; **23** there; **24** reason; **25** communicate; **26** ways

3.2 Student paper format, pages 19–23

It is important for students to learn about correct format and to master the vocabulary for talking about it. When they use good format, they can make a good first impression with their papers despite making language errors. Begin Activity A by telling the students that they are going to learn some important vocabulary.

With students' books closed, hold up a piece of lined paper for the class to see. Alternatively, either hold your book open to page 19 or display a transparency of the student paper on page 19. Briefly talk to the class about the parts of the paper, emphasizing the words *line, corner,* and *margin.* For example, *Here are the four corners of the paper. You write your name and the date in the upper right-hand corner. Here is the top line of the paper. What goes on the top line?* [The title.] *Here's another line. What's the name of this line?* [This is the left margin line.]

Then, have students open their books and repeat the words in the box after you. Ask which word(s) they can match with a number, and begin filling in the blanks together, starting with the known items, if any.

After the blanks are correctly filled in, have the students practice in pairs. Student A acts as the teacher and reads an item from the box. Student B, who covers the numbered list in her book, tries to say the correct corresponding number. Student A, who does not cover the list in his book, checks and says if the answer is right or not. After a minute, the students switch roles and continue the practice.

A Answers, page 19:

1 upper left-hand corner
2 top line
3 indentation
4 title
5 blank line
6 upper right-hand corner
7 lower left-hand corner
8 left margin line
9 bottom line
10 right margin
11 lower right-hand corner

For extra practice with the new vocabulary in Activities A and B, use a marker to write large numbers on a piece of lined paper to designate the parts that you want the class to review. Show the class the paper, and call out the name of a part. Students respond by saying the corresponding number.

C Possible answers, pages 22–23:

1 torn paper
2 incorrect left margin
3 incorrect right margin
4 incorrect indentations – too little, too big, too many
5 no title
6 no blank line after the title line
7 name in the wrong place
8 name signed and printed
9 no date

2
1 name in the wrong position
2 date in the wrong position
3 title not centered
4 title in all caps
5 title underlined
6 no indentation
7 unusual font
8 font size too big
9 text not double spaced
10 last sentence in italics
11 last sentence underlined
12 top margin too big
13 left margin too small
14 name in italics
15 date in italics

3.3 Independent-practice portfolio writing, page 24

There are several very workable topics here. You might enjoy assigning topics 2 and 3. They are easy for students to write about because they usually have strong opinions and lots of personal experience. Topic 4 is good because it will allow you to learn more about the hopes and aspirations of your students. Topic 5 is also good, but for a different reason. If you assign all students to report on the same event, their reports should contain the same basic facts even though they may express different opinions of the event. Therefore, you can compare their reports, or have them compare their reports, for completeness and factual accuracy.

In addition, this is a good time to have students turn to page 148 and begin work with the list of topics and the boxes to help them find a point of view or opinion about a topic. Have students brainstorm with the topics before having them begin to write.

Unit 4 Sharing Stories

Unit 4 is the heart of the book. The unit uses stories (narration), probably the most familiar genre of all, to introduce students to the full multi-draft composing process, quite possibly for the first time in English, perhaps for the first time ever. In the end, students turn out polished stories, based on their own experiences, for sharing and publication.

4.1 Talking about stories, page 25

This activity aims to stimulate discussion and heighten students' awareness of stories in their daily lives.

Possible answers, page 25:

1 by reading aloud from a book; through conversation; by reading aloud from a newspaper; by e-mail

4.2 Writing a story, pages 26–30

In these activities, students start getting ready to compose. They write out the story of the thwarted bank robbery, shown in the pictures on page 26, and master it through oral practice. Then they use this story to practice such things as using the past tense and adding details to prepare for working with their own stories later in the unit. In Activity A1, use the script on page 142 to keep your initial telling of the story simple and focused. In Activity C, it is helpful to show the story with blanks on a transparency or on big paper. As part of closure, do a chain telling of the story in which one student reads aloud one or two sentences, filling in the blanks, and then calls on another student to continue with one or two sentences, and so on. Then, give a couple of volunteers a chance to do the whole thing aloud by themselves. Usually one or two will give it a try while everyone else listens intently and helps if needed.

A Answers, page 27:

1 D-3
2 A-5
3 C-5
4 B-1
5 A-2
6 C-4
7 D-5
8 D-7
9 C-1
10 A-6
11 C-2
12 D-2
13 B-2
14 A-3
15 A-1
16 D-4
17 A-4
18 D-1
19 C-3
20 D-6
21 B-3

D Answers, page 29:

2 He gave the teller a note and got two bags of money from her.
3 She hit him hard with her umbrella and stopped him.
4 The woman had a handbag and an umbrella on her arm, and the boy had a balloon on a string.
5 He started to run away, but the woman quickly started to run after him.
6 A policeman immediately took the robber away, and a crowd watched.
7 The bank manager gave the woman a reward, so she looked very happy.
8 He gave the boy seven balloons, so the boy had a smile on his face.

E Possible answer, page 30:

See the story, "Quick Action," on page 31. This is essentially the story that students will write in this activity, except that the title will be "An Unsuccessful Crime," instead of "Quick Action," and the adjectives may be placed differently.

4.3 *Revising and editing,* pages 30–32

Here students continue to prepare for work with their own stories. In Activity A, students learn that the topic sentence of a paragraph in English may not necessarily be the first sentence. This information may stimulate students to start looking for topic sentences while reading in English for class and other purposes. They may become distressed when they cannot find topic sentences. You can use Activity N on pages 138–139 in the Mini-Handbook to show these students the common configurations, including the absence of a stated topic sentence when the main idea is implied. The fact that there may not be a topic sentence can be quite reassuring and liberating to the students as analyzers of English. You can also seize the opportunity to emphasize that as writers they should use topic sentences to make their writing clearer for readers.

A Answers, page 31:

2 **1** The stories have different titles. "Quick Action" has a topic sentence at the end. The adjectives may be included in different places.

2 "Quick Action" presents the main idea more clearly because it contains a topic sentence.

B Possible answer, page 31:

An Unsuccessful Crime

It was an ordinary day at the First National Bank. Everything seemed normal. An elderly man and his young granddaughter were in the bank. The man had an old briefcase and a new umbrella on his arm, and the little girl had a balloon on a long string. The man began to make a deposit and cash a check. Then a woman with a black-and-white hat walked in. The little girl saw the woman's picture on the wall and began to feel afraid. The woman slowly walked to a teller's window and suddenly pulled out a big gun. She gave the teller a note and got two heavy bags of money from her. She started to run away, but the man quickly started to run after her. He hit her hard with his umbrella and stopped her! A policeman immediately took the famous robber away to jail, and a crowd watched. The bank manager gave the man a reward, so he looked very happy. He gave the girl seven balloons, so the girl also had a big smile on her face. In the end, everyone was happy except the robber.

Activity C introduces editing symbols, the full list of which is in Appendix 4. Students should use this appendix throughout the course. Have them do the *Introduction to editing symbols* exercise at the top of page 149 to get them involved with this handy reference list.

C Answers, page 31:

1 A woman and her grandson were in the bank.
2 It was an ordinary day at the bank.
3 Everyone was happy except the robber.
4 The robber pulled out a gun.
5 The boy was also smiling. *Alternative answer:* The boy was smiling, too.
6 The woman had a handbag and umbrella on her arm.
7 The boy liked the balloon very much.
8 The robbery happened at the First National Bank yesterday.
9 The robber's hat was black and white.
10 He gave the boy some balloons.

4.4 Letters and e-mail, pages 32–33

These activities use students' mastery of the bank robbery story to review and extend work with letters and e-mail. Students often have fun identifying with and speaking for the characters in the story.

4.5 Your story and the composing process, pages 34–36

This is one of the most important parts of the course. It looks short but will take some time in several class meetings and may not be entirely finished for a few weeks. Here students and the teacher each choose a dramatic, exciting, important, and/or memorable personal experience to turn into a story to share and publish. The experiences of reading and talking about each other's stories and having one's story read are almost always engaging and strengthen the class' sense of community. Stories written by some of our students appear on page 20 and on pages 48–49. Reading them is a good way to begin your preparation for this part of the course.

The composing process is presented here in seven steps, explained in words, and illustrated in pictures. Start each step by using the picture to tell the class what you and they are going to do. Then, model each step by showing the class your work with your own story. Finally, finish up each step by referring back to the picture. Through demonstration and frequent reinforcement using the pictures, students will see what to do and begin acquiring the vocabulary for talking about the composing process.

In Step 6 on page 36, editing and writing the final paper can be accomplished in two ways. Use the method below that is compatible with your resources, but be aware that the cassette method may be preferable at this point in the course and more enjoyable to students because of the sheer number of small errors they are likely to make.

- The cassette-editing method requires that you or your students supply a 30-minute tape for each individual. The tape can be reused in upcoming units. Use this tape to record the second draft of the student's story. To do this, simply read the story on the tape in good English, correcting grammar mistakes, adding omitted details, and repairing organizational problems as you go. Use a slow but native speed. Do not break the work into phrase units because students will be able stop, rewind, and listen as many times as necessary. Return the cassettes with or without hand-edited papers. For homework, have students transcribe the recorded version of their stories.
- For the standard method of editing, simply mark the errors in their second drafts using the editing symbols with which they are familiar. Be selective about how many errors you mark so that students will not become overwhelmed and overly concerned about editing for perfect English. Focus on errors affecting comprehension, particularly spelling and verb-tense mistakes, omission of words such as subjects and verbs, and confusing word order. For homework, have students write a final draft of their story, stapling all prior drafts beneath the final version. You need to be able to compare both drafts to make sure the students have corrected all the errors in writing the final draft.

In Step 7, make a handout with a content question about each story for students to write an answer to as they read.

4.6 Thinking about the composing process, page 36

This activity is important in transforming the story-writing experience into a shared reference point. Use this activity to help students analyze what they did, learn the vocabulary for talking about it, and realize that it is important.

Units 5 through 14 offer many more activities for multi-draft composing. None, however, are developed in such concrete detail as these because you and your students will have these pictures and this shared experience to refer back to for guidance. Throughout the course, every time you work through a multi-draft sequence, we recommend that you bring students back to these pictures and steps on pages 34–36. Make connections between them and what the class is doing so as to reinforce the concepts and the vocabulary.

4.7 Independent-practice portfolio writing, page 37

The first two topics provide more opportunities for students to tell personal experience stories. The third topic is especially enjoyable for students to write and read. The fourth topic ties in with Unit 6 and the publication project.

Unit 5 Three Good Ways

Unit 5 is a continuation of the two prior units. It takes off where Unit 4 ends, in that students use the process approach to create a second multi-draft composition. It also continues where Unit 3 ends, in the sense that students write their own formal expository paragraph using enumeration signals.

5.1 Three ways of writing, pages 38–39

The three diagrams illustrate types of writing students have done in the previous units and will help them understand that different writing situations require different strategies. Students need to choose the best strategy for each circumstance. Begin by describing each one orally and letting students match your description with the picture.

- For timed writing, you might say, *This person has only a short time for writing, but he wants to organize the paper carefully. He makes a few notes before he begins writing, and he rereads and revises his work before the time is up.*
- For multi-draft writing, you might say, *This person has been working on an important paper for several days. After writing down his first ideas, doing some research, and discussing his ideas with another person, he writes a first draft. Then, he gets feedback from another person and possibly does more research before he works on writing a second draft. He makes changes and edits his work before writing his third and final drafts.*
- For one-step writing, you might say, *This student is probably writing a note to a friend or perhaps doing some independent-practice writing for a portfolio assignment.*

Answers, page 38:

1 One-step writing
2 Multi-draft writing
3 Timed writing

Possible answers, page 39:

2 **1** One-step writing: writing a letter to your family; writing a birthday card note; keeping a diary of your daily activities; writing directions for a friend
2 Timed writing: writing an essay for a history (literature, economics, etc.) examination; writing a TOEFL® essay; writing a GRE/GMAT essay; writing a job application essay; writing a last-minute report for your boss; writing a business letter
3 Multi-draft writing: writing a paper for your writing course; writing an important business paper; writing a research paper for a university course; writing a story for a contest

5.2 Independent-practice portfolio writing, page 39

The discussion of the topics is just as important as the writing. Allow plenty of time for pair and whole-class discussion before asking students to choose a topic for writing.

5.3 *Reading and editing,* page 40

Activity A reviews the content of Activities 5.1 and 5.2 and asks students to identify enumeration signals, which were introduced in Unit 3. Activity B provides practice with the editing symbols, with particular focus on the use of articles in enumeration signals, such as *the first way,* and the use of gerunds in transforming verbs into noun forms.

B Answers, page 40:

1 People have three good ways of writing.
2 The first way is writing only one quick draft.
3 The second way is planning, writing, revising, and editing several careful drafts.
4 People use this way when they write something important.
5 The third way is writing carefully in a timed situation, without help or feedback.
6 All three ways of writing are useful if people use them in the appropriate situations.

5.4 *Introduction to outlines and diagrams,* pages 41–42

This is a fun and simple introduction to planning good paragraph structure. Activity A1 is easy and quick to do because of the previous work with the same paragraph in Activity 5.3. Preview Activity A2 by asking students to tell you which ways they use to communicate with friends and relatives. Then, have them read Activity A2 to discover whether their ideas match the ways listed in the paragraph. Activity B introduces students to making a diagram, which is another way of showing paragraph structure.

A Answer, page 41:

2 Ways of Writing to Friends and Relatives

Topic: Three useful ways of writing to friends and relatives
- A. Writing letters by hand
- B. Writing e-mail messages
- C. Writing instant messages

B Answer, page 42:

2

5.5 *Introduction to formal style,* pages 42–43

In Unit 2, students learned about the importance of capitalization and punctuation, and in Unit 3, they learned a lot about the format of a student paper. Activities A and B in 5.5 continue the discussion of the conventions of writing and focus on the language of formal writing. Point out to students that although formal style usually avoids or limits the use of first and second person pronouns, it does not call for eliminating them altogether. Students can and should be encouraged to draw on their personal experience in giving support for their points when writing timed essays.

Activity B2 can be done orally if you read the situations and have students jot down their answers on scrap paper with their books closed. Then, students can compare answers with a partner and open the book to review and discuss situations about which they agreed or disagreed.

B Answers, page 43:

2

1 I	**5** F
2 F	**6** F
3 F	**7** F or I, depending on the teacher's instructions
4 I	**8** F or I, depending on the teacher's instructions

5.6 Formal style paragraph, pages 43–45

This sequence of activities will help students write their second multi-draft paragraph compositions and should be illustrated by referring often to the series of pictures in Unit 4 on pages 34–35. In Activity A, students brainstorm topics; in Activity B, they form opinions for topic sentences; and in Activity C, they plan their writing by outlining.

Activity D is best done in the classroom. It is useful to collect and read these first drafts before moving on to Activity E at the next class meeting. In this manner, you will know what kind of feedback to coach your students to give each other. Collect all materials again after Activity E so that you can make editing and revising suggestions for them to follow in Activity F.

In Unit 4, students share their stories; in Activity G, it is similarly important for students to share the final drafts of their formal, expository paragraphs. You can also write a list of questions for students to answer, one per paragraph, and then post the final drafts, gallery-style, around the classroom for reading. The questions can focus on content, organization, and even format.

Using the cloze practice procedure described in the notes for Unit 3 on page 8, you could prepare one or more cloze exercises, similar to the one below.

Three Ways of Sleeping in Class

According to many students, sleeping ________ (1) class is often necessary. There ________ (2) three easy ways to sleep in ________ (3) so that the teacher does ________ (4) notice. The first way is ________ (5) dark glasses. Both tinted glasses ________ (6) sunglasses work well. If sunglasses are ________ (7) permitted, glasses with a dark ________ (8) tint are effective. The second ________ (9) is hiding behind a book. ________ (10) way works best in reading ________ (11) or in other classes for ________ (12) sitting in the back rows. ________ (13) may require sliding down in ________ (14) chair a little. The third ________ (15) way for students to sleep ________ (16) class is supporting the head ________ (17) the arm. This way requires ________ (18) tabletop, desktop, or armrest for ________ (19) elbow to rest on. All ________ (20) ways are useful in different ________ (21) and usually prevent trouble with ________ (22) teacher.

 (135 words)

Possible cloze test answers: **1** in; **2** are; **3** class; **4** not; **5** wearing; **6** and; **7** not; **8** blue; **9** way; **10** This; **11** classes; **12** students; **13** It; **14** the; **15** easy; **16** in; **17** with; **18** a; **19** the; **20** three; **21** situations; **22** the

Unit 6 Class Publication

Unit 6 introduces students to the format and contents of newspapers and Web sites, making crossword puzzles, and beginning a class publication project.

6.1 *Types of publications,* page 46

With books closed, show a locally available English-language newspaper and find out if students are familiar with it. Write the words *newspaper* and *publication* on the board or a transparency, and make certain students understand that a newspaper is one type of publication. Have students brainstorm about other publications people use to share/publish information or stories for other people to read. Then, have students open to the illustration on page 46 and compare the class list of types of publications with the ones shown.

Possible answers, page 46:

2 **1** All are used to publish or share written materials, such as news, stories, and advertisements, and to display photographs and other types of visual information for a large number of people to read or see. The word *publish* and the words *public* or *publication* have the same root meaning: *people,* so the reason to publish is to involve many people. These publications differ in many ways, such as the technology used, the writers, the readers, the types of information included, the profit or nonprofit status, and the place where each might be found.

2 Reasons vary. Possible reasons include to sell ads and make money; to create a sense of community; to promote a cause, such as a healthier environment; to educate people; to give writers an audience for their work; and to entertain people.

3 Answers will vary.

6.2 *Newspapers,* pages 46–49

Begin Activity A1 by showing sample newspapers in English. Write their names and other vocabulary on the board or a transparency as they come up in the discussion, being sure to elicit some or all of the newspaper vocabulary in the questions in Activity A2. This discussion, though essential to the success of pair work in Activity A2, should be incomplete so that students do not know the answers to all Activity A2 questions before they begin.

In Activity A2, you can alter or add to the questions, if appropriate, in order to focus on additional parts, such as stock market or sports news, that might be of special interest to your class, for example, *Why do newspapers have advertisements?* [To pay expenses and make a profit. The price an individual pays for a newspaper covers only a small part of the actual production costs; selling ads pays for the rest.] Activity A2 works best if there is one newspaper per pair or small group, although the newspapers do not need to be the same or even current.

Activity B involves excellent hands-on learning and will produce useful displays for later use. It involves cutting up newspapers. If you prefer not to cut newspapers, simply have students look at a newspaper and identify samples of each item in the blue box. These can be photocopied for a later display. You can also use items from the sample student newspaper on pages 48–49. However done, Activity B is important in helping students to learn the terms in the box in Activity B and to learn to identify parts of a newspaper. Assuming authentic newspapers have been used in Activity B, Activity C will serve as a review and help students visualize how their own class newspaper might look.

C Answers, page 47:

masthead of the paper, advertisement, article about local news, weather report, headline

6.3 *Web sites,* pages 50–51

These activities are similar to the ones in Activity 6.2 and will familiarize students with the content and vocabulary of Web sites. Before beginning Activity 2, introduce some or all of these words: *Web address, banner, column,* and *link.* Activity 3 is a lot of fun if your class has access to the Internet. You can choose a Web site in class or have students suggest a variety of them to visit. This can be done in class or as a computer lab assignment.

Answers, page 50:

2
1. <http://www.ueng.edu/eng310/>
2. The Web page begins below the Web address. A banner is similar to a masthead of a newspaper, and this one includes an abbreviated version of the Web address, the name of the Web site, and a slogan "Read & Enjoy."
3. The information at the bottom includes the Web address of the publisher of this book and the e-mail addresses of the authors. In addition, the date of publication is printed here.
4. English 310 Showcase
5. Yes, June 1.
6. According to the first line, you would expect to see a collection of student writing.
7. The Web site has three columns. Column 1 lists the types of information while column 2 gives specific details about unit numbers and the names of the articles. Column 3 is an elongated box containing an advertisement about future additions to the Web page.
8. Columns 1 and 2 function as the menu.
9. Yes, the underlined text represents links, and column 1 contains links that readers can click to access different types of information.
10. Yes, column 3 is a type of advertising.

6.4 *Crossword puzzles,* page 51–52

Making crossword puzzles is fun but not as simple as it may appear. Activity B is great practice for WH-question formation, which may challenge even your abler students. In Activity C1, emphasize the instruction that *any two words touch in only one place.* This instruction keeps the puzzles from becoming much too hard. These student-made puzzles do not need to look like professional puzzles, in which almost every square is filled with a letter.

When students finish Activity C, you will have a nice collection of puzzles and a variety of ways to use them. Certainly, students should publish some in a class publication, but you can use others to provide extra work for fast-finishers or as change-of-pace work for the whole class. In addition, you can display a student's puzzle on a transparency and read (as you correct) the questions aloud for an interesting listening and spelling activity. (Some students may be motivated to ask to redo their puzzles carefully after they realize you are actually using them in class.)

6.5 *Independent-practice portfolio writing,* page 53

Since this is the fifth independent-practice assignment, it may be useful to have students look at their previous work and ask themselves whether they are making progress in terms of increased length, better format, number of ideas or details included, feelings of confidence about writing in English, and so on. Since there is little writing in Unit 6, this might be a good time to have students do two topics, one from the Unit 6 list and another from the list on page 148 in the SB, particularly if they have not used page 148 so far. The time might be right to ask students to review the entire contents of their portfolio. Have they completed everything assigned so far? Refer to the list on page 147 in the SB to identify the guided-practice portfolio assignments.

6.6 A class publication, pages 53–54

Most classes enthusiastically embrace the idea of making a class publication and offer many ambitious suggestions about its format and contents. Keep things as realistic and simple as possible, but don't be afraid to use the energy and talents of your students. Some students who may not particularly enjoy writing may become much more interested and involved in it if their technical, artistic, or organizational skills are also involved in the course.

We strongly recommend you create a first edition of a newspaper or Web site (or magazine or wall display) as early in the course as possible (perhaps now) rather than waiting until the end when schedules are hectic. As you can see from the sample student newspaper on pages 48–49, a class might enjoy an issue consisting almost entirely of their personal stories from Unit 4.

Part Two

Writing More, Writing Better

Unit 7 Follow These Steps

Unit 7 begins with a process dictation and asks students to share their expertise by describing a process that they already know.

7.1 Process dictation, pages 56–58

Students usually enjoy looking at driver's licenses and photographs and discussing the process of getting a license. You can have them locate Massachusetts on the map on page 123. Tell students that the name *John Doe* is often used as a typical or generic name in the United States when the real name is either unknown or unimportant.

Activity B is the second dictation sequence in the SB. If, for whatever reason, this is the first one you have used, read the two-paragraph overview in the notes for Activity 3.1 on page 6.

A Answers, page 56:

1 The pictures show three steps in getting a driver's license in Massachusetts.
2 Answers will vary. Most U.S. driver's licenses have the person's name, address, birth date, height, hair and eye color, and a photograph of the person's face.
3 Answers will vary.

C Answers, page 57:

1 A person can get a learner's permit at an earlier age and without knowing how to drive.
2 Parents usually supervise teenage drivers, but older brothers and sisters sometimes supervise, too.
3 According to the paragraph, the steps are 1) taking a course and written exam; 2) practicing under supervision; and 3) taking a driving test. Ask students which part of step 1 from the dictation is not pictured.
4 Answers will vary. Here are two useful Web sites.
U.S. states: <http://www.du.edu/psychology/frs/resources.htm>
Europe: <http://www.encyclopedia4u.com/d/driver-s-license.html>

(2) **1** The topic is the process by which a teenager can get a driver's license in the United States.
2 first sentence
3 last sentence
4 A *process* means a procedure, a method, a way, or a series of steps.

(4) The signal words are *three basic steps, first, next, finally,* and *three-step process.*

D Answer, page 58:

Steps in Getting a Driver's License

In the United States, teenagers can get a driver's license before becoming 18 by following three basic steps. First, they get a learner's permit by taking a course and a written exam on traffic laws. Each state has a driver's handbook for learners to study. Next, they practice driving under adult supervision, usually with parents or older siblings. This step is very important in learning practical skills. Finally, they take a driving test for a regular license. The hard part of this test is parallel parking. Following this three-step process allows U.S. teenagers to drive at a young age.

7.2 Revising process paragraphs, pages 59–60

The paragraph in Activity A contains errors caused by mixing the chronology and enumeration signals shown on the file card on page 57. Students can rewrite using either set of signals. Although other combinations of signals exist, a fact that some students are quick to point out and that should be readily acknowledged, it is helpful to insist students master the grammar of these two sets before embracing other variations.

The Activity B paragraphs illustrate how simple processes can be made to seem very complicated by overuse of signals. The point here is for students to practice combining many small steps into basic (major) steps that are easy for the reader to understand and remember.

These activities can be completed along with the brainstorming, outlining, and planning steps that open Activity 7.4, where students explain their own process in three basic steps.

A Answers, page 59:

2 The first box below shows the revision with chronology signals. The second box shows the revision with enumeration signals.

Getting a Driver's License

There are three easy steps in getting a new driver's license. First, people study the rules in the driver's handbook carefully. Next, they go to the driver's license office to take the written test. Finally, they take the driving test. People who follow these three steps can get a driver's license quickly.

Getting a Driver's License

There are three easy steps in getting a new driver's license. The first step is studying the rules in the driver's handbook carefully. The second step is going to the driver's license office to take the written test. The third step is taking the driving test. People who follow these three steps can get a driver's license quickly.

B Answers, pages 59–60:

1 The topic is my grandfather's disgusting dish and how he made it.
2 Topic sentence: *It did not have a name, but here is his process.*
3 There are nine steps.
4 Steps 1, 2, 3, 4, 6, 8, and 9 have one sentence each; steps 5 and 7 have two sentences each.
5 Concluding sentence: *This dish was unforgettable because it looked so disgusting that no one would eat it, except my grandfather.*
6 Many good titles are possible, including "A Disgusting Dish," "My Grandfather's Cooking," "How My Grandfather Made a Bad Dish," "Cooking Without a Recipe," and so on.

2 **1** same answer as B1, answer 1 above
2 same answer as B1, answer 2 above
3 There are four steps.
4 Steps 1 and 4 have one sentence each; steps 2 and 3 have two sentences each.
5 same answer as B1, answer 5 above
6 same answer as B1, answer 6 above

3 Possible answer, page 60:

> The Composing Process
>
> Careful writers use a seven-step composing process to produce good work. First, they collect ideas, make a plan, and write the first draft. These steps are usually easy when the topic is familiar or interesting. Then, they revise their work and write a second draft. These steps require making changes by adding, deleting, and reorganizing information before writing a second draft that shows the changes. Finally, editing before sharing is important because most writers make small errors in spelling, grammar, and punctuation that need to be corrected. Some of these steps can take much longer than others do, and repeating steps is common. Following this seven-step process consistently can help improve anyone's writing.

7.3 Editing, pages 60–61

A Answers, page 60:

1 **1** Careful writers want to produce good work.
2 They follow these steps.
3 Before sharing their work, they edit it carefully.
4 The composing process has seven steps.
5 The first step is collecting ideas and writing the first draft.
6 There are seven steps in the composing process.
7 Following this process can improve my writing.

B Answer, page 61:

> The Composing Process
>
> Careful writers use a seven-step composing process to produce good work. First, they collect ideas, make a plan, and write the first draft. Then, they revise their work and write a second draft. Finally, before sharing, they edit for mistakes. Some of these steps can take much longer than others do, and repeating steps is common. Following this seven-step process consistently can help improve anyone's writing.

7.4 Publication project: How-to Guide, pages 61–62

This set of activities leads students to use the full composing process, which is illustrated on pages 34–35. With these aids, students can produce a paragraph explaining a process they know well – possibly an everyday process known by all. Alternatively, they can explain a specialized process with which they are familiar, but which would be of interest to all.

7.5 Independent-practice portfolio writing, page 63

These topics provide additional practice describing people (Units 1 and 2), telling personal stories (Unit 4), and explaining a process (Unit 7). Assign some topics for homework and do some in the computer lab if possible. Good format (Unit 3) and standard paragraph organization should be expected. More proficient students may be able to write more than 200 words. For TOEFL®-type practice, allow 30 minutes, and aim for more than 200 words.

Unit 8 Class Statistics

Unit 8 introduces students to very simple numerical data, such as averages and ranges, and guides them to use these basic statistics as factual support in two paragraphs, first about the English class in the book and then about their own class. This unit can help draw in students who find working with numbers and calculation more appealing than writing. Specific suggestions are given for adapting Activity 8.5 for classes that are highly homogeneous, with everyone of the same age, from the same country, and so on.

8.1 Class data and statistics, page 64

Introduce the unit by telling your students that they are going to be writing about classes – an English class in the book and their own class. Begin Activity 8.1 by giving an observation test about the picture. Follow the general observation-test procedure given in notes on Activity 1.1 on page 1; however, instead of asking students to give immediate oral responses, have them write *True* or *False* on scrap paper.

Questions for True-False Observation Test:

1 *The picture shows people in a hospital.* [False]
2 *There are only men in the picture.* [False]
3 *You can see a door in the picture.* [True]
4 *There are more than six people in the picture.* [True]
5 *You can't see any chairs in the picture.* [False]

Check the answers, and give students another five-second observation period.

Questions for the second round of the True-False Observation Test:

6 *The ages of the students are listed under the picture of the class.* [True]
7 *One student is wearing a baseball cap, and another is wearing glasses.* [True]
8 *One student has his hands in his pockets.* [True]
9 *There are two open books on the table.* [False]
10 *No one in the picture is bald.* [False]

Then, elicit answers to the questions given in the book.

Answers, page 64:

1 50%
2 16
3 55
4 From 16 to 55
5 28.7 years

2 Some possible answers are math, health, biology, and economics.

8.2 Math terms, pages 65–68

The actual math here is simple, but the goal is to give students lots of practice in hearing a variety of numbers in English, pronouncing them correctly, and using the right terminology when reading problems aloud. For Activity A, instructions for extra oral practice are given in the script in Appendix 2 of the SB.

B Answers, page 65:

2 **1** Ten plus seven equals seventeen. *Alternative answer:* The sum of ten and seven is seventeen. (addition)
2 Four times five equals twenty. (multiplication)
3 Thirty-six divided by three equals twelve. *Alternative answer:* Three into thirty-six equals twelve. (division)
4 Eleven minus two equals nine. (subtraction)
5 Fifty divided by five equals ten. *Alternative answer:* Five into fifty equals ten. (division)
6 Eighteen thousand times one equals eighteen thousand. (multiplication)

C Answers, page 66:

2 **1** One point five plus two point two five equals three point seven five.
2 Two point five minus one point three equals one point two.
3 Zero point five times zero point three equals zero point one five.
4 One-half plus one-fourth equals three-fourths. *Alternative answer:* The sum of one-half and one-fourth is three-fourths.
5 Two minus two-thirds equals one and one-third.
6 Five divided by one-half equals ten. *Alternative answer:* One-half into five equals ten.

D Answers, page 66:

2 **2** Six-ninths equals two-thirds. Two-thirds is equivalent to sixty-six point six percent.
3 Nine-tenths is equivalent to ninety percent.
4 Three-fourths is equivalent to seventy-five percent.
5 Ten percent of twenty-five equals two point five.
6 Fifty percent of twenty-five equals twelve point five.

Activity E uses concrete, easily-demonstrated content to introduce the format and terminology for tables, which will be useful for students as they read and do research in English. Before class, copy (or have a student copy) Table 1 on page 67 on the board or a transparency to use during the activity. (The drawings can be very rudimentary!) Introduce *width, height,* and *depth* by measuring two or three of the students' book bags with a tape measure or ruler. In Activity E2, ask for a volunteer or two to fill in the table on the board or transparency while the other students fill in the missing information in their books.

E Answers, pages 67–68:

4 **1** weight
2 range; 13
3 height
4 range; $15.00; $55.00
5 in; from; to

5 **1** Average width: 15.75, which rounds to 15.8"; Explanation: 1) Add the widths of the bags: 18 inches plus 15 inches plus 17 inches plus 13 inches. The sum is 63. 2) Count the number of bags. There are four. 3) Divide 63 by 4. This equals 15.75. This number rounds to 15.8. The answer is 15.8. (For some classes, you will need to write the explanation on the board as an example for students to follow as they explain the remaining items.)
2 Average height: 12.5" (Explain as in 5.1.)
3 Average depth: 5.375, which rounds to 5.4"
4 Average weight: 1.6875, which rounds to 1.7 lbs.
5 Average price: 28.4975, which rounds to $28.50

8.3 *Organizing data into a paragraph,* page 68–70

In Activities A–C, students prepare to write a guided-practice paragraph for their portfolios in Activity D. Activity A gives practice with some of the headings that students will use when doing their own survey later in the unit. It also exposes them to vocabulary and sentence structures they can use in the later paragraph about their own class.

B Answers, page 69:

② **1** Sentences 1, 3, 4, 6. We consider the best order to be the one shown in the paragraph in Activity D below. It arranges these sentences from general/big to specific/little. Perhaps you and your class can defend a different arrangement as being better.

2 Sentences 2, 5, 7, 8, 9. Again, we think the best order is shown in the paragraph in Activity D below, but you and your class may come up with a defensible order that you think is better.

3 We put the sentences about *home countries* before the sentences about *situation now* because of chronology. The students lived in their home countries first, so these sentences go first. Also, the information related to students' home countries is part of their basic identification information and is often used first when they meet someone new. The exception is sentence 7. Although the class that it mentions is part of the *situation now,* this sentence "defines" the class and thus directly supplements the topic sentence.

C Answers, page 69:

Sentence 2

② Sentence 1

(Note: The other sentences may be useful to your students in Activity 8.5 on page 71 if you have a homogeneous class.)

D Possible answer, page 70:

Meet Writing 310

The Writing 310 class in the English Program is varied and interesting. The class consists of ten students; half are males, and half are females. They come from six countries in Africa, Asia, North America, and Europe. They speak the following native languages: Japanese, Spanish, Russian, French, and Swahili. These students come from cities and towns that range in size from 1,000 to four million people. In their countries, they had a variety of occupations. For example, four were students, one was a mechanic, and another was a doctor. The students have been here for varying lengths of time. One student has been here for two years, and another student has been here for only one week. The average length of time here is 5½ months. The students range in age from 16 to 55 years. Their average age is 28.7. Sixty percent of the students are married, and forty percent are single. Three students live alone, and one student lives with a roommate. The other sixty percent live either with their spouses and/or with relatives. All in all, the Writing 310 class is very diverse and fascinating.

(188 words)

8.4 *Revising and editing,* pages 70–71

Remind the class that these activities will help them get ready to work with their own writing. Have students turn back to pages 34–35 and look again at the pictures of the revising and editing steps. Very briefly review what revising and editing are and where they fit in the overall composing process.

Activity A can be challenging in terms of content and keyboarding but also quite engaging. The key is the warm-up. Write "California" on the board. Ask students to just raise their hands in answer to such questions as, *Has anyone been to California? Can you find California on a map?* Then, have the class turn to the map on page 123 and find California. Ask such questions as, *What is the capital of California? Can you name other cities in California? What states are near California? Look at the map of the United States. Is California one of the bigger or smaller states? What country borders California? What ocean borders California? What things do tourists like to see and do in California?* Also, if you have been to California, you can tell the class about your trip(s).

Next, have students look at the scrambled California paragraph in the box on page 70. To give everyone a chance to hear and say the words, read each sentence aloud and then have the class read it aloud along with you. Ask a quick question about the sentence (e.g., *What is the percentage of Hispanics in California? How much of the population is under the age of 18?*) before moving on to the reading and choral repetition of the next sentence.

Finally, help the class answer the questions in the book. As part of homework or computer lab work, you may want to ask students to look at the Web site mentioned in the paragraph and write two more facts about California to turn in and/or share with the class.

A Answers, page 70:

1. According to the 2000 U.S. Census, California has a population of more than 33,871,000.
2. Sentences 4 and 10 together function as the topic sentence. Sentence 4 gives a reason for writing about the topic, and sentence 10 names it. The concluding sentence is 8.
3. Population statistics about 1) the whole population; 2) gender; 3) age; and 4) ethnic groups
4. See the order of the sentences in the A2 paragraph below. The data is arranged from more general to more specific.

2

California in 2000

Few visitors to California know many statistics about the state. According to the 2000 U.S. Census, California has a population of more than 33,871,000. This makes it the most populous state in the United States. The population has grown 13.6% since 1990. Just over half of the population is female. About a quarter of the population is under the age of 18. One tenth is 65 years or older. Among the many ethnic groups in California, the largest groups are whites (59.5%), Hispanics (32.4%), Asians (10.9%), and blacks (6.7%). The smallest reported group is Native Hawaiian and Other Pacific Islanders (0.3%). Visitors who are interested in more statistics about California can find them at http://quickfacts.census.gov/gfd/states.

B Answers, pages 70–71:

1. These students come from four different continents.
2. Forty percent of the students are married, and 60 percent are single.
3. Ten students, three women and seven men, are in this English class.
4. This class has an economist, a civil engineer, a lawyer, a computer scientist, and six students who are working on their degrees.
5. The students range in age from 20 to 33 years, and the average age is 26.5.

8.5 Composition, pages 71–73

This survey is great fun. Your students will enjoy the tangible process of making the data collection sheet and collecting data. Begin by reading the article called "Meet Level 2A" in the sample student newspaper on page 48 in the SB and/or the following alternative paragraph, which provides an example of a paragraph about a homogeneous class of students all from the same country.

Meet Section 7B English

The students in the Section 7B English class are alike in several ways but have some interesting differences in their experiences and preferences. The class consists of 25 female students. All were born in Japan and speak Japanese as their native language. However, only 78 percent of the students were born in this city. The others were born in towns and cities that range in size from 1,500 to 20 million. All of the students have studied English for six years in school, but only 55 percent have studied English outside school. Only 16 percent have visited an English-speaking country. The students take varying lengths of time to get to school. The maximum length of time is 1 hour and 7 minutes, and the minimum is 9.5 minutes. The average length of time is 35.6 minutes. In the future, the students want to work in various occupations. For example, six students want to work in marketing, four want to be accountants, and three want to start their own businesses. The students also prefer to visit different continents. Their top choices in decreasing order are Europe (36%), South America (20%), Africa (16%), Australia (12%), North America (12%) and Antarctica (4%). All in all, the students in Section 7B English have a lot in common, but they differ in some interesting ways.

 (220 words)

In Activity A1, brainstorm about types of data your class would like to collect, incorporating most or all of the ideas in the box. After deciding on six additional, appropriate headings for the survey, you can give students a blank sheet of unlined, and perhaps colored, paper. Have them fold their paper lengthwise several times to form enough rows for the students in the group. Then have them refold the paper crosswise to form enough columns for the nine headings you have chosen. This will form a blank grid for the headings, questions, and data.

If your students are similar in terms of the same origin, age, marital status, and reason for learning English, you can substitute some or all of these headings (and associated survey questions).

- Name and size of birthplace (What town or city were you born in? About how big is/was it?)
- English study outside school (Have you studied English outside school? If so, how long have you studied?)
- Length of time in an English-speaking country (Have you visited an English-speaking country? If so, which one? How long were you there?)
- Length of time to get to school (How long does it take you to get to school?)
- Future occupation preference (What job do you want to have in the future?)
- Continent preference (What continent do you want to visit the most?)

Before Activity A4, have the class practice asking the questions aloud several times before forming small groups for the actual survey.

A Answers, page 71:

3 You can often think of more than one way to frame a question for a given heading, but here is one set of possibilities: What did you do in your country? What country are you from? What's your hometown? How big is it? What continent are you from? How long have you lived here? (How long have you been in this school/program?) How old are you? How long have you been studying English? Are you married? Why are you learning English?

After compiling data in Activity B, students must use the data as the basis for a composition in Activity C. Follow the steps in the composing process, as presented in Unit 4, pages 34–35, to develop, revise, and edit this composition.

Using the cloze practice procedure described in the notes for Unit 3 on page 8, prepare one or more cloze exercises, similar to the one below.

Meet Section 7B English

The students in the Section 7B English ________ (1) are alike in several ways but ________ (2) some interesting differences in their experiences ________ (3) preferences. The class consists of 25 female ________ (4). All were born in Japan and ________ (5) Japanese as their native language. However, ________ (6) 78 percent of the students ________ (7) born in this city. The others ________ (8) born in towns and cities that range ________ (9) size from 1,500 to 20 million. ________ (10) of the students have studied English ________ (11) six years in school, but only 55 ________ (12) have studied English outside school. Only 16 ________ (13) have visited an English-speaking country. ________ (14) students take varying lengths of time ________ (15) get to school. The maximum length ________ (16) time is 1 hour and 7 ________ (17), and the minimum is 9.5 minutes. ________ (18) average length of time is 35.6 ________ (19). In the future, the students want ________ (20) work in various occupations. For example, six ________ (21) want to work in marketing, four ________ (22) to be accountants, and three want ________ (23) start their own businesses. The students ________ (24) prefer to visit different continents. Their ________ (25) choices in decreasing order are Europe (36%), ________ (26) America (20%), Africa (16%), Australia (12%), North America (12%) and Antarctica (4%). ________ (27) in all, the students in Section 7B English ________ (28) a lot in common, but they ________ (29) in some interesting ways.

 (223 words)

Possible cloze test answers: **1** class; **2** have; **3** and; **4** students; **5** speak; **6** only; **7** were; **8** were; **9** in; **10** All; **11** for; **12** percent; **13** percent; **14** The; **15** to; **16** of; **17** minutes; **18** The; **19** minutes; **20** to; **21** students; **22** want; **23** to; **24** also; **25** top; **26** South; **27** All; **28** have; **29** differ

8.6 Independent-practice portfolio writing, page 73

Topic 4 in particular often stimulates interesting pieces of writing and gives students an opportunity to use enumeration in conjunction with description and/or narration. For TOEFL®-type practice, allow 30 minutes, and aim for more than 200 words.

Unit 9 The Perfect Routine

Unit 9 uses the concrete topic of daily routines as a means for working with complex sentences and adding sensory details. First, students write one paragraph using information from a classmate who then gives feedback. Then, they write another paragraph using their imagination to interest and entertain their classmates.

9.1 Ms. Lee's daily routine, pages 74–75

Before class, you may want to make a transparency or enlarged copies of the 16 picture cues to display as prompts for closed-book oral practice and testing.

Activity A serves as an excellent introduction to the concept and vocabulary of a common daily routine. Activity B, done in depth, ensures that students master the daily routine sentences before forming complex sentences in Activity 9.2. In Activity B, have students work independently at first to fill in the blanks. After a couple of minutes, pair the students so they can finish and compare answers. If necessary, interrupt the individual or pair work to reread the sentences to the class one or more times.

After checking, have pairs/triads of students drill each other. Student A in the pair/triad acts as the "teacher" and keeps the book open to both pages 74 and 75. Student B/C is the "student" and looks only at the pictures on page 74. Student A calls out the number of a picture and checks the sentence that Student B/C says for that picture. After a few minutes of practice, the students switch roles.

As closure for the oral practice, with books closed, display or point to the enlarged picture cues you have made, and ask for volunteers to say the corresponding sentences. For homework, have students memorize the sentences in Activity B by doing the following several times: look at the pictures, write the corresponding sentences, and check that they have written them correctly. In the following class meeting, test memorization by displaying the picture cues, saying the numbers in random order, and asking students to write the corresponding sentences on a piece of paper. Collect and check the work.

B Answers, page 75:
- See the script for Activity 9.1 in Appendix 2 of the SB.

9.2 Complex sentences, pages 75–77

Before starting Activity A, with books closed, use an overhead transparency or display your picture cues, from Activity 9.1 above, to demonstrate combining sentences with *before* and *after* and forming questions and answers. Then, have students open their books and practice with the exercise. Finally, have students perform with their books closed, possibly in a game format in which teams take turns asking each other questions. Give points for correctly formed questions and answers.

Before starting Activity B1, practice simple and compound sentences by working through Activity J and Activity K on pages 135–136. In conjunction with Activity B2, use the punctuation exercises in Activities P2–P5 on pages 140–141. As a supplement, if your class is ready to go deeper, do further work with complex sentences and subordinate clauses using Activity L and Activity M on pages 137–138.

B Answers, page 76:

2

2 She makes her lunch because she wants to save money.
(S V ... S V)

3 While she makes her lunch, she listens to the news.
(S V ... S V)

4 When she gets off the bus, she stops at a stand to pick up coffee.
(S V ... S V)

5 Before Liz has her lunch, she does paperwork.
(S V ... S V)

6 Liz's daily routine is very helpful although it is often boring.
(S V ... S V)

Possible answers, pages 76–77:

4 Sentences 4 and 5 require free responses. The rest draw directly on the 9.1 materials.

4 Although Liz uses a computer at work, she does not use one at home.

5 Because Liz works out at the gym, she looks great.

Activity C is challenging and interesting. Here are some ways to help students do a good job: Work with punctuation exercises in Activities P2–P5 on pages 140–141 if you haven't used them already; add the word *early* to the first picture cue; and encourage students to vary their sentences by following the guidelines below.

- Don't use the same sentence pattern more than twice in a row.
- Don't use the same adverbial conjunction more than twice in a row.
- In some sentences, put two or three verbs in a clause.
- When a given sentence about Liz's routine has a compound verb, try putting one of the verbs in a different clause or sentence if you want to.
- Consider including a simple sentence or two.

You may wish to read aloud one of the paragraphs below to give students an idea of what to do. You can even conduct the activity as a grammar dictation in which students take notes as you read and then work in pairs using their notes to reconstruct the paragraph as best they can.

C Possible answers, page 77:

Since there are many ways to form complex sentences using the given material, correct answers will vary. This is one possible correct version.

Liz's Weekday Routine

Liz Lee is a busy person with a useful daily routine. After Liz gets up at 5:30 A.M., she takes a shower and gets dressed. She listens to the news while she makes her lunch, and then takes the bus to work. After she stops at a stand to pick up coffee and a snack, she gets to the office, says hello, and checks her e-mail. She does paperwork and goes to meetings before she has lunch at her desk. She works at her computer and sees clients before she returns telephone calls. After she gets off work at 5 P.M., she gets together with friends or works out at the gym. When she goes to bed about 10 P.M., she dreams about the weekend and her next vacation. Liz's weekday routine is often monotonous, but it helps her deal with her busy life.

Below is another possible version, presented as cloze practice, in which two simple sentences are used along with the complex ones to give more variety. (For notes on using cloze, see Unit 3 on page 8.)

Liz's Weekday Routine

Liz Lee is a busy ______(1) with a useful daily routine. ______(2) gets up at 5:30 A.M. ______(3) she takes ______(4) shower, she gets dressed. She listens to the news ______(5) she makes her lunch. She ______(6) at a stand to pick ______(7) coffee and a snack after ______(8) takes the bus to work. ______(9) she gets to the office ______(10) says hello, she checks her ______(11), does paperwork, and goes to ______(12). She has lunch at her ______(13). She works at her computer ______(14) sees clients before she ______(15) telephone calls. When she gets ______(16) work at 5 P.M., she gets ______(17) with friends or works out ______(18) the gym. About 10 P.M. she goes ______(19) bed and dreams about the ______(20) and her next vacation. Liz's ______(21) routine is often monotonous, but ______(22) helps her deal with her busy ______(23).

 (146 words)

Possible cloze test answers: **1** person; **2** Liz; **3** After; **4** a; **5** while; **6** stops; **7** up; **8** she; **9** After; **10** and; **11** e-mail; **12** meetings; **13** desk; **14** and; **15** returns; **16** off; **17** together; **18** at; **19** to; **20** weekend; **21** weekday; **22** it; **23** life

9.3 Editing sentence structure, pages 77–78

These activities introduce the final three editing symbols that appear in the complete list in Appendix 4. Activity A shows students one way to deal with each of three common mistakes. In Activity B, however, one run-on, one fragment, and one comma splice are better corrected by compounding than by the ways shown on the file card. Thus, you can help students see that they cannot mechanically correct errors of these types in one prescribed way. They have to consider the meaning and context as they edit their writing.

A Possible answers, page 78:

1 She picks up a snack before she gets to the office.
2 Her job is busy, but she likes it. *Alternative answer:* Her job is busy. She likes it.
3 After she works out in the gym, she goes to bed early.
4 Her daily routine is boring, so she wants to change it. *Alternative answer:* Her daily routine is boring. She wants to change it.
5 She leaves work at 5 P.M. because she wants time to work out.

B Possible answer, page 78:

> Liz's Weekday Routine
>
> Liz is a busy person, so her daily routine helps her a lot. Every weekday, she wakes up at 5:30 A.M. After she gets dressed, she listens to the news while she makes her lunch. Then, after she takes the bus to work, she stops at a stand to pick up coffee and a snack. After she gets to the office and says hello, she checks her e-mail before she does paperwork and goes to meetings. She has lunch at her desk. Next, she works at her computer and sees clients. Before she leaves the office, she returns telephone calls. After she gets off work at 5:30 P.M., she gets together with friends or works out at the gym. She usually goes to bed at 10 P.M. and dreams about the weekend and her next vacation. Liz's weekday routine is often monotonous, but it helps her with her busy life.

9.4 Composition: A routine day, pages 79–81

In Activity A1, if the class has an odd number of students, make one triad of strong, motivated students who work quickly. Explain (before class, if possible) that they should try to do three interviews in the time that everyone else is doing two, and get them settled first. In the triad, Student A closes the book and gives answers. Student B asks the questions while Student C takes notes, asking for clarification as needed. Then, students rotate roles twice. If necessary, have them finish up as part of their homework, in person or by phone. As with the pairs, the note takers use their notes to write the compositions; thus, A writes about B, and B writes about C, and C writes about A. This procedure ensures that everyone's routine will be the subject of a composition. Another good alternative is for you to partner with a very low student. This will not only even the numbers but also give you an opportunity to help a low student build confidence.

A Possible answers, page 79:

2 monotonous, boring, difficult, hard, unusual, crazy, typical, useful, enjoyable, healthy, exciting

Activity C is designed to elicit more development and detail, regardless of the amount already present in any given draft. Students at this level almost always need to practice saying more. If you wish, you can have them analyze the sample paragraph, "Leo's Daily Routine" on page 34, before working independently.

Leo's Daily Routine

Leo Yang is a student with a consistent weekday routine. Leo wakes up every day at 8 A.M., but he always listens to the radio for about 15 minutes before he gets out of bed. After he eats breakfast and gets dressed, he leaves home at 9:45 A.M. He always takes the shuttle bus to school. On the bus, he sits quietly and thinks about his day for about 20 minutes. He starts classes at 10:45 A.M. on MWF and at 1 P.M. on TTh. He is always on time for his classes. At school, he studies English very seriously and takes a few breaks for lunch and in the afternoon. He gets out of school at 4:30 P.M. on MWF and 3:15 P.M. on TTh. He usually goes directly home after school, but on Thursdays he plays badminton at the school gym from 4 to 6 P.M. Leo always takes the bus home and cooks dinner as soon as he gets home. He usually eats dinner at 7 P.M. and eats out about twice per week, especially on Thursdays after badminton and on Saturdays when he has free time. In the evening, Leo swims in the pool at his apartment and does his homework. Before he goes to bed, he takes a shower. He usually goes to bed at 2 A.M. and sleeps only 6 hours. He goes to sleep at once and often dreams. He rarely remembers his dreams, but he knows they are sometimes nightmares. Leo thinks this consistent routine is very useful for his busy life.

 (260 words)

C Answers, page 80:

1. before school: 6 actions
2. at school: 4 actions
3. at home: 2 actions
4. in the evening: 4 actions

In Activity D, the act of marking in the partner's book lends weight to the practice. If you think that your students will be unduly influenced by seeing the writer's answers, have them cover both answer columns with folded paper (or an index card) on which they write *Partner's answers.* Then, ask them to slide the paper over just enough to write these answers in the book without uncovering the *Your answers* column. Explain that honest answers will help their partner, and assure them that they will have a chance to talk together about any differences. Then, help students follow the steps in the composing process, as presented in Unit 4, to revise and edit this composition.

9.5 Publication project: A perfect routine, pages 82–84

Students usually find this composition quite engaging, and they like reading about the teacher's perfect routine as well as those of their classmates. Take advantage of this enjoyable opportunity to share your own imaginative letter with the class.

9.6 Independent-practice portfolio writing, page 84

Give students the experience of focusing on their strengths rather than on their errors and weaknesses. Highlight two or three good sentences in independent-practice pieces of each student, or circle the good sentences in pencil and put a star in the margin beside them. Ask students to read the marked sentences silently, and decide which one to read to the class. Then, have each student read the chosen sentence aloud to the class. The reading takes only a few minutes but can be quite powerful.

Unit 10 Great Trips

Unit 10 takes students on one or more class trips – either in the real world and/or in cyberspace. If feasible, a real trip is much more rewarding than a virtual trip because of all the opportunities for incidental language learning that happen during the trip. Arrange trips according to your schedule, or coordinate with other classes or school activities. Students might do one trip early in the course and another trip at a later time.

10.1 A virtual trip, pages 85–86

Internet access is necessary for this activity, but it can be done equally well during class time or as an out-of-class assignment, either alone or in pairs or small groups. It can also be done more than once, using different Web sites each time. It is a research activity, designed to prepare students for more sophisticated research in future courses. You can put more or less emphasis on the research and documentation aspect. With an academic group, adding work with APA or MLA guidelines on citing Internet sources can be a useful expansion activity.

Because Web sites can become out-of-date, visit each Web site and correct or supplement the list on page 85 as needed. Be sure all additional Web sites are in English to enhance the language-learning experience. In Activity C, students must use either chronology or enumeration signals to write their reports.

10.2 A real trip, pages 87–89

Many schools and language institutes plan field trips for students or allow teachers to do so. Use these activities in conjunction with any scheduled trips. Whether you go on a trip as a class or not, students can read and fill in the class report entitled "Level Two at Met and Park" on page 48 as class work or homework. If a class trip is not permitted, students can take a trip on their own, with a partner, or with family members or friends. Or, students can recall a field trip or family trip that they have taken in the past. The best event, however, is a real class trip that is planned, taken, and written about as a group.

Activity C is a mystery game that requires writing or drawing during the trip. Bring pencils and activity forms if your chosen venue is appropriate for this game. (In some cases, you can have the students do the writing or drawing in the classroom sometime after the trip.) Before the matching step, it might be best if you type or write out the names of the objects so that students cannot use handwriting as the basis for matching.

Activity D works very well when the questions are presented in strip-story fashion, although you can certainly do it by referring students directly to the box on page 88 since the questions there are not in any logical order. For the strip-story procedure, modify the questions to suit the actual trip, write each question on a strip of paper, fold the strips, and put them in an envelope or basket. Have students close their books, draw one strip at a time, and read the question aloud to the class. Have the class answer each question aloud, providing as much help as necessary. (The activity can be made more difficult by not having the students write the answers.)

The interesting part of the composition process is deciding how to organize the information logically because some questions imply chronological order and some do not. Therefore, the revising step in Activity E is very interesting and can yield some excellent variations. Overall, follow the steps in the composing process, as presented in Unit 4 and pictured on pages 34–35, to develop, revise, and edit this class trip composition.

Activity F encourages publication of the finished compositions. In addition to the ideas on page 89, another possibility is to review letter-writing skills, and rewrite the compositions as the body paragraphs of a letter to the director of the institute or school or even as a letter to a friend. Page 5 shows a model of a good letter.

10.3 Independent-practice portfolio writing, pages 89–90

The first three topics continue the theme of the unit while the fourth and fifth ones preview Unit 12, which explores the theme of exercise and the use of reasons as support for an opinion.

Unit 11 Info Expo

This unit contains a dictation that teaches how to write a paragraph of classification. It continues by having students choose a class theme for an Info Expo (Information Exposition) and write individual classification paragraphs related to this theme. The photos on page 96 illustrate the topics some students chose for the theme of "Environmental Problems."

11.1 Classification dictation, pages 91–93

This dictation about three main *types* of dictionaries builds on two prior dictations: three *ways* of staying in touch in Unit 3 and three *steps* in getting a license in Unit 7. It can be done much earlier than the Info Expo compositions as an easy introduction to the concept of classification.

This is the third dictation sequence in the SB. If, for whatever reason, this is the first one you have used, read the two-paragraph overview in Activity 3.1 on page 6.

Begin with a short observation quiz. After students study the photo on page 91 for ten seconds, have them close their books and answer these questions orally: *Are all the books the same? Are all the books in English? How many books are in the photo?* Then, have students open their books and answer the printed questions with a partner. If your students have electronic dictionaries, be sure to talk about them.

C Answers, page 92:

1. Answers may vary, but the meaning and pronunciation are usually included.
2. The definitions will vary according to the dictionary used. The point of this question is to have students actually use their dictionaries and compare the information they find.
3. Answers can vary, but the class should discuss the ideas that they will eventually encounter in the supporting sentences in Activity D on page 93.
4. Answers will vary.

(2)
1. The topic is types of dictionaries.
2. The final sentence is the concluding sentence.
3. This is a classification paragraph with enumeration signals.

It is important for students to understand that the dictation in the box is really a very poor paragraph because it contains no details about the three types of dictionaries. To make it complete, interesting, and detailed, supporting information must be added. Consequently, Activity D is very important.

D Answer, page 93:

Advice about Dictionaries

People studying English usually want a good dictionary. There are three main types to consider. One main type is a bilingual dictionary. It translates words from English into another language, and vice versa. Another main type is a dictionary for learners of English. It has easy definitions and special information, such as example sentences and usage notes, for people learning English. For example, it tells whether a noun is count or noncount. Still another main type is a dictionary for native speakers of English. It includes old forms of words and historical information about them, so it is sometimes difficult to understand. Therefore, before buying, students should think carefully about which of these three main types is best for them because each type serves a different purpose.

11.2 Reading and outlining, page 94

Ask students to brainstorm on the topic of different types of student housing and what they know about each type before they open their books to read the paragraph. After they outline, have students pay particular attention to both the classification signals, which provide the skeleton; and the supporting sentences, which provide the meat of the paragraph. This paragraph, which contains 132 words in 8 sentences, is well developed compared with the dictation paragraph on page 92, which has 61 words in 6 sentences. Discuss with students that the difference is not just how many sentences are included but, more important, how many interesting details are included in each sentence. Students who are planning to take a TOEFL® test or other placement test in the future need to be reminded that the way in which an essay is developed is usually an evaluation criterion.

Answer, page 94:

2 Topic: Popular types of student housing

A. Dormitories
B. Apartments
C. Cooperative houses

11.3 Revising and editing, pages 94–95

Begin with a discussion of types of computers and their characteristics and uses. The point of Activity A is for students to develop this paragraph by adding details from their own experiences and knowledge.

Activity B classifies Web sites as personal, commercial, and informational. Begin with a discussion of different types of Web sites as a warm-up and have students compare the classifications that they think of with the three types presented here. After they read, help students evaluate this paragraph carefully and come to the realization that it not only needs editing, but also lacks good development. For example, ask them: *How many words are there?* [About 80.] *How many sentences?* [Eight, after editing.] *Are there topic and concluding sentences?* [Yes.] *Are there enough organizational signals?* [Yes.] *Is there enough development?* [No.]

The paragraph contains a wide variety of error types. After making corrections, students can be asked to add three supporting sentences – one for each type of Web site – in order to develop the paragraph further and increase its length. The following possible answer shows the corrected paragraph with additional sentences for further development.

B Possible answer, page 95:

Common Types of Web Sites

Web sites can be divided into three common types. One common type is a personal site. Individuals use this type of site to share photos with friends. It saves paper and is much faster and more economical than sending ordinary photos to several people. Another common type of Web site is a commercial site. Businesses can use this type to sell or advertise products or services. For example, airlines sell tickets and issue boarding passes on their Web sites. Still another common type is an informational site. Universities, government agencies, and organizations use this type to provide information to the public. For instance, universities provide semester calendars, course schedules, and application forms online. These days, most people use all three types of Web sites and rely on them more and more every day.

(133 words)

11.4 Publication project: Info Expo, pages 95–98

Give students a five-second observation test on the photos on page 96 and ask them the questions in Activity A1 on page 95. (You might want to refer to the procedure for this type of activity in the notes to Unit 1 on page 1.) Write the words *Info Expo* on the board and ask students if they know the full words. While the term *exposition* may not be familiar to students, most of them have probably attended an exposition, fair, or industry show some time in their lives – perhaps a book fair, an agricultural exposition, or a study abroad fair. Refer to local events that are most familiar to your students and talk about the fact that each exposition has a theme related to an activity, industry, or product.

Use Activity B to begin planning an Info Expo for your class. Overall, use Activities B–D to carry out the steps in the composing process, as presented in Unit 4 and pictured on pages 34–35, to develop, revise, and edit compositions for the Info Expo. Although the activities on pages 96–98 do not mention research, classes that need to develop research skills can use the library or Internet to gather details on their topics. High-proficiency, academic classes can create a reference list of sources they use in writing.

In addition to the publication ideas on page 98, students might also make posters and invite other classes to visit and ask questions. These additional activities will provide a listening-speaking activity that will reinforce the writing process – and provide a real-life experience for your class and other classes to write about.

11.5 Independent-practice portfolio writing, page 98

Once again, give students the experience of focusing on their strengths rather than on their errors and weaknesses. Follow the instructions in the notes for Activity 9.6 on page 34.

Unit 12 Exercise Opinions

The title of Unit 12, *Exercise Opinions*, has the intentional double meaning of "opinions about exercise" and "exercise your opinions," depending on whether you interpret *exercise* as a verb or an adjective, in order to summarize the double purpose of the unit. Students do a sentence-combining activity about exercise in the workplace, work on a dictation about why people exercise, and write paragraphs that express and support opinions about the popular theme of exercise and sports.

12.1 *Getting some exercise,* pages 99–100

The drawings and activities introduce the theme of the unit. Note that the drawing on the right depicts a floor aerobics exercise. Other examples of aerobic exercise are running, brisk walking, step aerobics, cycling, cross-country skiing, dancing, and swimming.

With some classes, you may find it most effective to do the stretching activity with books closed before students open their books and answer the first set of discussion questions. In addition to getting students out of their desks for a welcome change of pace, the stretching activity introduces some useful vocabulary items.

The vocabulary that students study in the "Ergonomic Workstation Checklist" on page 100 and the discussion questions in the final part of Activity 12.1 prepare students for the sentence combining in Activity 12.2.

Answers, page 100:

4
1. *Ergonomic* means designed to be maximally safe, comfortable, and efficient.
2. Answers will vary.
3. Exact answers can vary. In general, stand and stretch regularly and often. Also, shift often and maintain good posture while sitting. To avoid headaches and eyestrain, do regular and frequent eye exercises such as alternating your focus on objects that are near, at a medium distance, and far away.
4. Sit as shown in the drawing of the ergonomic workstation.

12.2 *Sentence combining,* pages 100–101

Activity A, which involves listening twice to the combined paragraph with books closed, is essential in preparing students for the sentence combining in Activity B. After finishing Activity A but before beginning Activity B, your class should review the punctuation of compound and complex sentences as shown on the file cards on pages 29 and 76 and as practiced in Activity P4 on page 141.

Activity B, which provides practice in writing longer sentences, is a satisfying, engaging exercise that produces a well-developed paragraph. The key to doing it well is the preparatory listening and oral practice. Once the paragraph is written, be sure that students note the deductive-restatement organizational pattern with the topic sentence presenting an opinion supported by three detailed examples.

B Possible answers, page 101:

Use the paragraph given in the script in the SB on page 145.

12.3 Dictation: Why people exercise, pages 102–104

This is the fourth dictation sequence in the SB. If, for whatever reason, this is the first one you have used, read the two-paragraph overview on page 6.

The second question in Activity B1 asks students to distinguish between fact and opinion. Use this as a simple preview to Activity 12.6, which continues this topic. For the moment, you can have students look up the two words in their bilingual dictionaries if confusion arises.

B Answers, pages 102–103:

1 For their cardiovascular health, for their appearance, and for fun and relaxation

2 Sentence 1 asks a question. Sentences 2, 3, 4, and 5 express facts. Sentence 6, which is the topic sentence, expresses the opinion. Here, *in fact* means "in conclusion."

3 *Cardio* means the heart; *vascular* refers to the network of vessels (arteries and veins) for the circulation of blood.

4 **a** potato; **b** pizza; **c** cup of milk
Note: If your students have access to the Internet, have them predict the answers and then check by going to <http://www.google.com>, <http://www.askjeeves.com>, or another search site. They can type in *calories in common foods* or *calories in a potato*, etc., to find facts such as these:

- Potato, boiled, medium: approximately (~) 88 calories
- Tomato, medium: ~ 20 calories
- Individual salad of 2 cups lettuce and 2 tablespoons oil-based dressing: ~ 180 calories
- Pizza, slice, ¼ of 9-inch cheese-and-tomato pie: ~ 195 calories
- Pizza, slice, ¼ of 9-inch pepperoni, cheese, and tomato pie: ~ 260 calories
- Milk, whole, cow's, 1 cup: ~ 156 calories
- Coffee, black, percolated, 1 cup: ~ 5 calories

2 **1** The topic sentence is the last sentence. Yes, it expresses an opinion.
2 Enumeration is used.
3 Reasons that people exercise is what is being enumerated.

4 The Set A enumeration signals are used. The signals used are *some, other,* and *still other.*

In Activity C, you may want students to discuss the fact that the finished paragraph has only minimum support and that, by adding additional facts or personal experiences, they could develop it more fully. If time allows, have them add additional supporting facts, either personal experiences or facts discovered through a survey or Internet research.

C Answer, page 103:

Why People Exercise

Why do people exercise? People exercise for many different reasons. Some people exercise for their cardiovascular health. They want to build strong hearts and circulation. Other people exercise for their appearance. They try to burn more calories because they want to lose weight, look better, and build firm muscles. Still other people exercise for fun and relaxation. They enjoy themselves when they exercise. In fact, most people probably exercise for all three reasons.

12.4 *Reading about reasons,* page 104

Before opening the book, have a conversation with the class. Ask such questions as *Which sports do you like to participate in? Which sports do you like to watch on television? Are some sports better to watch on TV than others? Why do you think so? Are some sports better to watch on TV than in person? Why do you think so?*

Answers, page 104:

1 The topic is why football is successful on U.S. television.
2 The main purpose is to express an opinion about reasons that football is successful on U.S. television.
3 The writer gives three reasons with facts and examples to support each reason.

2 Topic: Three reasons that football is successful on U.S. television

A. Football has lots of action.
B. Viewers can actually see the game better on TV than in person.
C. Football is good for advertising.

12.5 *Revising and editing,* page 105

A Possible answer, page 105:

Reasons to Exercise

People exercise for three different reasons. The first reason is to improve cardiovascular health. People want to build strong hearts and circulation. The second reason is to improve appearance. People try to burn more calories because they want to lose weight, look better, and build firm muscles. The third reason to exercise is to have fun and relax. People enjoy themselves when they exercise. In fact, most people probably exercise for all three reasons.

B Answer, page 105:

Reasons for Going to a Gym

Different people go to a gym for different reasons. Some people go to a gym to work out with weights. Other people go to a gym to take exercise classes in aerobics or yoga. Still others go to a gym because they can meet new people and make friends outside work. There are other reasons for going to a gym, but these are three important ones.

12.6 *Fact and opinion,* pages 105–106

Fact, opinion, truth, untruth, real, unreal, convincing evidence, inadequate evidence are terms that can be the subject of deep philosophical debate. However, since your students may not yet have the proficiency for such a discussion, keep things basic. A *fact* is something that we accept as true because of objective, positive proof. An *opinion* is what someone thinks or believes is true. To be accepted, an opinion needs to be supported by facts.

A Answers, pages 105–106:

Topic sentences should express an opinion while supporting sentences should present facts (statistics, examples, or experiences) that support the opinion. An opinion that is limited and focused can usually be supported by facts that are objective and provable; however, an opinion that is too broad, or too general, cannot.

2 Column A expresses opinions, but they are too broad and cannot be supported by facts. Column B expresses opinions that are appropriately limited and can therefore be supported by facts. Because they are very limited and easily supported by facts, they may be misinterpreted as facts. In column A, students should do the following.

- Circle *All* and *boring*. These words make this opinion too broad to be supported by facts. For example, soccer is a sport, and some people think that it is very interesting.
- Circle *Everyone* and *should*. These words make this opinion too broad to be supported by facts. For example, we can think of this exception: People who have a high fever should not exercise.
- Circle *best*. Again, this is an opinion that is too general because different people have different ideas about what is the best exercise for them.

3 **1** O This is an opinion that can be supported by factual conclusions from medical studies.
2 O This opinion is so well supported by data and so well accepted by people that it may seem to be a fact.
3 O This opinion can be supported by data on the number of football teams in the United States, players' salaries, ticket sales, and so on, as well as by personal experiences of people who are football fans or who live with fans.
4 O This opinion can be supported by statistics as well as personal experiences.
5 O This is a well-limited opinion and can be supported by examples.
6 O This is an extremely broad opinion and would be difficult to support by facts. For example, there are many other ways to get enough exercise, such as playing sports, walking in the neighborhood, and so on.

12.7 Opinion publication, pages 106–107

Look out for magazines and newspapers that contain both invitations to readers to submit their opinions and pieces written by readers. Many publications feature a regular letters-to-the-editor section. *Newsweek* magazine, for example, also includes "My Turn," a one-page essay by a reader. If possible, briefly show the class an authentic request and/or reader response before focusing on Activity A. As you move through the activities in this composition sequence, use the pictures on pages 34–35 of the SB to remind the students of where they are in the composing process.

Have students write their first drafts in class or as homework. Follow the steps in the composing process, as presented in Unit 4, to develop, revise, and edit this composition.

12.8 Independent-practice portfolio writing, page 108

Topics 1 through 4 ask students to express an opinion. They will provide additional practice in stating reasons and providing support with facts, examples, or personal experiences.

Unit 13 Portraits of Special People

Unit 13 prepares students to write a paragraph about someone special for sharing in a class portrait gallery, whether via a wall display, booklet, magazine, newspaper, or Web site. In the paragraph, students focus on three good qualities of the chosen person and use examples as support.

13.1 Portraits, pages 109–111

Introduce Activity A by giving an observation test on the picture of the gallery. Follow the general observation-test procedure given in Unit 1 notes on page 1, but have students write their answers of *True* or *False* on scrap paper.

Questions for True-False Observation Test:

1. *The picture shows people looking at paintings, possibly in a museum.* [True]
2. *There are only women in the picture.* [False]
3. *In the picture, you can see several paintings on the wall.* [True]
4. *The paintings are landscapes, that is, scenes of the outdoors showing mountains, lakes, and trees, and so on.* [False]
5. *One of the people in the picture is in a wheelchair.* [True]

Check the answers and give students another five-second observation period.

Questions for the second round of the True-False Observation Test:

6. *The people in the paintings on the wall don't look very important.* [False]
7. *All of the museum visitors are wearing glasses.* [False]
8. *None of the museum visitors is wearing a dress.* [True]
9. *One of the museum visitors is making notes.* [False]
10. *When you look at the picture, you don't see anyone who is bald.* [False]

Check the answers. Then, elicit answers to the questions given in the book.

A Answers, page 109:

① **1** Portraits are paintings, drawings, or photographs of a person, especially those of the person's face. They can also be verbal or written descriptions of a person.
2 A gallery is a building or hall where artistic work is displayed.
3 Answers will vary.

② **1** The types of people that are seen in portraits are important, famous, interesting, good-looking, and/or rich people; for example, political leaders, heads of organizations and companies, artists, and movie stars.
2 Artists and photographers make portraits to capture something of the personality or character of the people in the portraits and show it to viewers, especially future viewers.
3 People are fascinated by other people and their clothes, customs, and surroundings. People are also fascinated by the abilities of artists to make art by showing (painting, drawing, sculpting, photographing) a person of interest.

Begin Activity B by giving examples of special people from your own life. Then, choose one to describe orally to the class here and write about later for the class gallery. Students will delight in knowing about someone special to you, and your details will help them fill in the blanks appropriately. Before going on, have students make a firm decision about which special person they have chosen because they will write about this person in Activity 13.3.

In Activity C, have students identify the topic sentence that expresses the opinion (sentence 2) and the many small facts used to support each quality.

C Answers, page 111:

2 **1** *Quality* means a feature or characteristic that distinguishes or identifies someone.
2 She describes three qualities: love of learning, ability to cook everything well, helpful to everyone.

3 *one; another; still another*

13.2 *Personal qualities,* pages 111–112

In these activities, students use information about Thomas Edison to practice giving examples as factual support in illustrating personal qualities.

Build interest by asking, *How many lightbulbs are there in this room? Is it (are they) incandescent or fluorescent? Who invented the incandescent lightbulb?* If appropriate, for class work or homework, you can have students do some Internet research about Edison and/or the invention of the lightbulb.

Next, have the class look at the photo of Edison on page 111. In talking about it, you may want to explain that many people of several nationalities, including Canadian, English, French, and Russian, invented lightbulbs. Furthermore, many of them did so before Edison did. However, some historians give Edison credit for inventing the incandescent lightbulb because he designed his bulb as part of creating the whole electrical system for entire cities rather than just as a laboratory experiment or for an isolated room or house. Furthermore, through his money and power, he actually implemented his system.

Make sure students understand that Activity A presents opinion sentences that can probably be supported by facts. Activity C asks students to match qualities (i.e., opinion statements) with the relevant concrete example (i.e., facts). Students will need to understand this distinction to write the composition in Activity 13.3.

A Answers, page 111:

- adj One good quality was that he was creative/curious/determined/energetic/self-confident.
- n One good quality was his creativity/curiosity/determination/energy/self-confidence.

B Answers, page 112:

2
- *plays piano at a community center* – helpful to others, kind, active in the community
- *called her at midnight to ask a question* – supportive, understanding, not easily angered
- *loaned me some money* – generous, understanding, loyal
- *volunteered to help me with a big project* – generous, loyal, helpful, supportive
- *makes beautiful wooden gifts* – talented, patient

3
- her love of learning (For example, after she finished all eight grades at her rural school, she took a one-month course in teacher training.)
- her ability to cook everything well (Without written recipes, she made delicious bread and desserts, such as fruit pies.)
- her helpfulness to everyone (Many times she helped her neighbors with the hard parts of their sewing.)

C Answers, page 112:

1 f	**5** d
2 g	**6** e
3 c	**7** b
4 a	

13.3 *Portrait composition,* pages 113–115

You can make these activities clearer and more interesting for your students by sharing qualities, examples, an outline, and a first draft about the special person you chose in Activity 13.1B. Use Activities D and E to help students practice the revising and editing process. The paragraph in Activity D, for example, lacks appropriate enumeration signals – a problem some of your students may have. Activity E reviews a wide variety of mistakes and editing symbols.

D Possible answer, page 114:

A Great Friend

Kyle Robertson, my best friend from childhood, has three good qualities that I admire. The first quality is his energy and sense of adventure. One time, we visited his grandparents in Georgia. Another time, we went to see my uncle in San Francisco. Many times, we went skiing, backpacking, or rock climbing together. A second quality is his technical skills. For example, in junior high, we spent hours at the computer as "pilots" of simulated planes and, in high school, flew remote-controlled planes. Now we enjoy different activities, such as building Web sites and editing videos together. A third good quality is that he is loyal. He is always there for me, no matter when or where. For instance, I recently needed last-minute help at 4:00 A.M. with an important Java assignment. There was no problem when I telephoned and woke him up, and he had an answer to my question, as always. In short, Kyle has many good qualities and is really a special friend.

(166 words)

E Answer, page 115:

A Wonderful Friend

Rick Porter, my close friend and neighbor for many years, has many good qualities. One good quality is his delightful sense of humor. For example, he always has a new joke to tell at parties. Even if he makes a mistake when he is telling the joke, he can still make everyone laugh. Another good quality is that he is interested in new things. For example, if he hears a new song that he likes on the radio, he calls and asks the disc jockey for the name of the CD and details about the artist. One time, when he heard about a new type of Honda, he investigated it on the Internet, contacted a local dealer, and took a test-drive as soon as the new models arrived. Still another good quality is his open-minded friendliness. He likes to meet new people, on the beach, in the gym, or at a friend's dinner party, and finds the best in everyone. People like him because he is tolerant of people's lifestyles, interested in their hobbies, ready to talk about any topic, and rarely critical of anything. These three good qualities make Rick a special person and wonderful friend.

(197 words)

13.4 *Publication project: Portrait gallery of special people,* page 116

If you choose to make a wall display, invite others (another class, other teachers, the director, friends) to take part in the reading activity. You might also publish and share these essays by having students rewrite them as cloze exercises. (For cloze exercise information, see page 8.)

13.5 *Independent-practice portfolio writing,* page 116

Have students compare how much and how well they can now write in 15 or 20 minutes with how much they could write at the beginning of the course. There is usually quite a lot of improvement.

Unit 14 An Armchair Visit

This unit contains a dictation and asks students to write both a one-paragraph travel essay and a multi-paragraph essay on the same topic. Classes may do both essays or just one of them, as is appropriate for their level and proficiency. Students may engage in a lot of research or very little, depending on the goals of the course. With higher proficiency, academic classes, there is a great opportunity for writing a sophisticated, researched paper.

14.1 Dictation: The proud state of Texas, pages 117–120

This is the fifth dictation sequence in the SB. If, for whatever reason, this is the first one you have used, read the two-paragraph overview in the notes for Activity 3.1 on page 6. If possible, make an audio recording of the dictation instead of reading it aloud. Note that this is the longest, and perhaps the hardest, dictation in this book because it contains a lot of supporting details. Note also that the dictation contains several numbers, some of which are spelled out. Review the basic rules for writing numbers with words or numerals in the notes for Activity 1.2 on page 1.

Activity A1 begins with a quick observation task that is fun to do. Most students enjoy drawing. It focuses attention and provides humor and discussion even if the products are not very good. For Activity A2, students can refer to the U.S. map on page 123. You can also draw a compass on the board to teach or review the words *north, south, east,* and *west.*

A Answers, page 117:

2
1 Texas is in the south central part of the United States.
2 Texas borders the country of Mexico.
3 **a** Oil wells can be found near Amarillo.
b Rice fields can be found on the Gulf of Mexico.
c Cattle ranches can be found in West Texas.
d Pine forests can be found in East Texas.
e Oranges and grapefruit can be found in South Texas.
f Space research takes place at NASA in Houston.
4 Answers will vary.

C Answers, page 118:

1 Texas is famous for its oil wells, ranches, cowboys, and size.
2 It takes about twelve hours if you are going about 70 miles per hour. Its greatest length, from north to south, is 801 miles (1,289 kilometers). The state's greatest width is 773 miles (1,244 kilometers).
3 *Upset* means "unhappy."
4 Texas became second to Alaska in size.
5 mainly ice

2
1 The size of Texas is the topic of the dictation.
2 The second sentence is the topic sentence.
3 *Size* is the key word. Other related words, which create coherence, are *large, the largest, the biggest.*
4 Yes, the last sentence.

4
1 The anecdote in the dictation is the joke (a funny story) that Texans told about Alaska being made mainly of ice.
2 This anecdote is used to support the topic of the size of Texas.

Activity D (see also Activity C2.3) asks students to identify synonyms and focus on the idea that you sometimes have to rephrase a sentence when you use different words.

D Answer, page 119:

> The Proud State of Texas
>
> Texas is known everywhere for its oil wells, cattle ranches, and cowboys. It is also well known for its size. In fact, Texas is so large that it takes about twelve hours to drive across it. For 114 years, Texas was the largest state in the United States. In 1959, however, Alaska became the forty-ninth and largest state. Proud Texans did not like this at all, so they joked that since Alaska was mainly ice, it could melt. In their opinion, Texas remained the biggest state.

F Answers, page 120:

(1) **1** Because of its size, it takes about twelve hours to drive across the state.
2 Alaska became the forty-ninth and biggest state in 1959.
3 Texas is famous for cowboys and oil.
4 Texans are always joking about Alaska because it is mainly ice.
5 It takes almost twelve hours to drive from East Texas to West Texas.
6 Texas borders four other states, which are Louisiana, Arkansas, Oklahoma, and New Mexico.
7 Texans are proud of their state.
8 Texas is an interesting place to visit.

14.2 Paragraph to essay, pages 120–122

This activity expands students' knowledge of Texas beyond the dictation. Both the paragraph and the essay focus on the three less well-known points about Texas: its geography, cultural heritage, and strong pride.

A Answers, pages 120–122:

1 Texas has interesting features other than cowboys and oil wells.
2 The three points are varied geography, cultural heritage, and regional pride.
3 The concluding sentence restates the idea of the topic sentence using different words and specific features.

(2) **1** Topic sentence: 1
2 Sentences about geography: 2, 3, and 4
3 Sentences about cultural background: 5, 6, and 7
4 Sentences about regional pride: 8, 9, 10, 11, 12, and 13
5 Concluding sentence: 14

B Answers, page 122:

(2) **1** Introduction: 1
2 Body: 2, 3, and 4
4 Conclusion: 5

(3) Both the last sentence of the introduction and the first sentence of the conclusion give the main idea of the essay.

(4) varied geography; cultural heritage; regional pride

(5) **1** The first anecdote is in the introductory paragraph.
2 The purpose of the first anecdote is to introduce the topic.
3 The second anecdote is in paragraph 4 and was also presented in the dictation.
4 The purpose of the second anecdote is to support the third topic of Texas pride.

14.3 A travel paragraph, pages 123–125

A higher proficiency class can do Activities 14.3A and B only – before going directly to Activity 14.4. Lower groups may do only Activities 14.3A, B, and C and omit Activity 14.4 completely.

In Activity A, you may wish to focus your students on a particular region and begin with a map of that region. Otherwise, let students explore many regions and maps before making any decisions. There are many possibilities, so allow students as much input as possible.

Form a team for each region chosen, and make sure each individual chooses a different place within the region. In this way, students can collaborate, perhaps use the same resources, and yet write individual paragraphs. (If one region is especially popular, more than one team can work on it.) It is important to have each team and each individual commit to a specific area and a specific place. Have students write their choices both in the blanks at the top of page 124 and on a small piece of paper to turn in to you. When choices have been made, you can more easily provide materials or direct students to useful resources.

While some teachers may be able to provide the reading materials about the places chosen, library and/or Internet research will help students learn about the place they will be writing about. If students are doing independent research, they should print or photocopy the things they read so that you may also read them. If appropriate for the class or curriculum, these materials provide useful practice in paraphrasing correctly to avoid just copying sentences and phrases. This is a great place to introduce the concept of plagiarism.

After researching and reading, students should plan their paragraphs by deciding which features are well known and which are interesting but not well known. The model paragraph about Texas focuses on less well-known features, and students can follow this model or focus on well-known features, according to your best judgment based on the places chosen.

After students write their first drafts, have them staple all their research materials to the draft for you to review. Follow the steps in the composing process, as presented in Unit 4 on pages 34–35, to develop, revise, and edit this composition.

14.4 Travel paragraph to essay, pages 125–128

These activities ask students to expand their one-paragraph essays into five-paragraph essays. To begin, have students read the essay on page 121 and complete the outline on page 125. Be sure to discuss the format of a formal outline, which uses roman numerals, capital letters, periods, and internal vertical alignment.

Students must use their notes from Activity 14.3B on page 124 to begin the tentative outline of their essays on page 126. You can expect this outlining activity to reveal the need for more research and reading on one or more of the interesting features in the body paragraphs.

Have students do Activity C and write their introductory paragraph while they finish their research. If feasible, students can write both types of introductions and get feedback from you and/or a partner before deciding which one to use. Because the introduction should be a full, well-developed paragraph, students may need to add supporting details and write a second draft of it.

When the research is finished, have students finish the outline on page 126 and use it as a guide to writing the body paragraphs. Students can write all the body paragraphs before revising and editing, or they can write, revise, and edit each body paragraph separately. Either method will work well.

Finally, have students do Activity D and write a relatively simple concluding paragraph, which restates and continues the ideas in the introduction, and does not present any new details.

Then, have students combine all the paragraphs to form one essay, which should have at least two to two and a half pages of text, totaling about 750 words, with each paragraph being one-third to one-half page long. Have students reread their own essays and prepare final, typed versions of their outlines from page 126 to turn in along with their papers.

Revision and editing are very important steps because the final essays will be interesting to share and read. Each team can make a small booklet for classmates. Or, essays can be posted on a bulletin board or published on a class Web site. To develop public speaking skills, students can also give speeches, or teams can make oral panel presentations about their places. If students need to prepare for the TOEFL® writing, this multi-draft essay can be a good beginning point.

A Answer, page 125:

2 Outline

I. Introduction
II. Varied Texas geography
    A. Geographical features
    B. Climates and plants
III. Cultural background of Texas
    A. Past cultures
    B. Present culture
    C. Future culture
IV. Regional pride of Texans
    A. Texas products
    B. Texas history
    C. Texas size
V. Conclusion

14.5 Independent-practice portfolio writing, page 128

Some classes enjoy making a souvenir audiotape in which each student reads a favorite independent-practice selection.

Appendix 1 The Mini-Handbook

A The alphabet, page 129

This is an important reference section for students who have trouble forming the letters of the alphabet or making their capital letters distinguishable from their lowercase letters. It is also an important review section for almost everyone. Even students who can rapidly write and say the alphabet usually need to 1) review the pronunciation of some letters, such as *e, g, i, j, k, q,* and *z*; 2) learn to ask *Excuse me, how do you spell . . . ?*; and 3) practice writing down words spelled to them orally at a native pace. Useful related expressions to teach with reference to e-mail addresses are *in all caps, all lowercase,* and *case sensitive.*

B Parts of speech, page 130

Although *speech* refers to oral production, the term *parts of speech* is the traditional name for the grammatical labels used to identify types of words, whether spoken or written. Be sure that everyone learns the abbreviations because they will be used along with editing symbols to help students correct their work. You can make a matching exercise for introduction or follow-up by listing the parts of speech and scrambling their definitions.

B Answers, page 130:

Answers will vary.

2
1 Ouch! (interj.); foot (n.); really (adv.)
2 and (conj.); are (v.); in (prep.)
3 A (art.); mine (pro.); interesting (adj.)
4 had (v.); bad (adj.); dream (n.)
5 often (adv.); dream (v.); about (prep.)

C Phrases, page 131

Recognizing phrases can help students learn to identify and to avoid fragments in their own writing. Students work further with phrases in Activity D and with prepositional phrases in Activity J2 on page 135.

C Answers, page 131:

The format of my first paper was bad. I did not put the title in the center of the top line. I started a sentence in the left margin. I wrote my name at the end of the paragraph and put the date under it. Because of these mistakes, I got a bad grade in format.

2

An ordinary, elderly woman stopped the famous robber. She got a large reward, and her young grandson got seven big balloons. In the end, everyone was happy, except the unsuccessful robber.

3

Today isn't a good day. We do not have time for lunch. We also do not have time to check our e-mail. We wanted a better day. Tomorrow is going to be better.

D Sentences, pages 131–132

Students are introduced to the concept of sentences in Activity 2.5 of the SB on pages 12–14. There they identify subjects and verbs. Here they distinguish between sentences and phrases.

D Answers, page 132:

1. S
2. S
3. P (subject needed)
4. S
5. P (verb needed)
6. S
7. P (subject and verb needed)

E Sentences with linking verbs and subject complements, page 132

In these sentences, the verbs link the subject with a subject complement, which completes the subject by describing or explaining it.

E Answers, page 132:

1. Fred (s); was (v); a bad cook (sc)
2. he (s); became (v); a chef (sc)
3. he (s); appears (v); comfortable (sc)
4. dishes (s); look (v1); beautiful (sc1); taste (v2); delicious (sc2)
5. Everyone (s); feels (v); happy (sc)

Possible answers, page 132:

2
1. Green tea is a healthy drink from Asia.
2. Green tea has become popular in North America.
3. Green tea tastes delicate and fresh.
4. The carpet in the new apartment seemed a good choice for families with young children.
5. The carpet in the old apartment smelled awful.

F Sentences with *There is/are* and *Here is/are*, pages 132–133

F Answers, page 132:

1. types (s); are (v)
2. restaurant (s); is (v)
3. restaurant (s); is (v)
4. directions (s); are (v)
5. menu (s); is (v)

Possible answers, page 133:

2
1. There are several big cities in my country.
2. There is a movie theater near here.
3. There is some broken glass in the street.
4. Here is a photo of my family.
5. Here are my sister and her new baby.

G Sentences with direct objects, page 133

G Answers, page 133:

1. people (s); use (v); computers (do)
2. students (s); do (v1); research (do1); write (v2); papers (do2)
3. family (s1); friends (s2); professors (s3); send (v); e-mails (do)
4. everyone (s); plays (v); game (do)
5. Computers (s); serve (v); functions (do)

Possible answers, page 133:

2 1. Last night Pat and Kim watched <u>movies</u> for hours.
2. They saw <u>four movies</u> between 6 P.M. and 2 A.M.
3. On weekends, they rent <u>horror movies</u>.
4. They invite <u>several friends to watch these movies with them</u>.
5. Together they eat <u>popcorn</u> and drink <u>lemonade</u>.

H Gerunds and gerund phrases in sentences, pages 133–134

This is good to use in conjunction with the Unit 3 dictation on pages 15–18.

H Answers, page 134:

1. Swimming (gerund, subject)
2. Swimming laps (gerund phrase, subject)
3. swimming laps (gerund phrase, object of a preposition)
4. swimming laps (gerund phrase, direct object)
5. Swimming (gerund, subject)

2 staying in touch (object of a preposition); writing letters (subject complement); making phone calls (subject complement); sending e-mail messages (subject complement)

I Forms that function as subject, subject complement, and objects, page 134

I Answers, page 134:

1. Austin (s, N); is (v); the music capital (sc, NP)
2. Listening to live music (s, GP); is (v); popular in Austin (sc)
3. Musicians (s, N); enjoy (v); playing in Austin (do, GP)
4. *South by Southwest* (s, N); is (v); a popular music festival (sc, NP)
5. Many music lovers (s, NP); attend (v); this festival (do, NP)
6. Listening (s, G); is (v); a real pleasure (sc, NP)

Possible answers, page 134:

2 1. Music <u>is an important part of life for many people</u>.
2. Classical music <u>usually takes time to learn and appreciate</u>.
3. It <u>often stirs our emotions</u>.
4. Listening <u>can be a pleasure or a challenge</u>.
5. Playing the violin <u>takes practice</u>.

J Simple sentences, page 135

Simple sentences are important in writing strong, clear English – at both basic and sophisticated levels. Simple sentences can be rich in information because of compound subjects and/or verbs or through the addition of prepositional phrases that expand meaning. It is very important for students to master the concepts of simple sentences and of compound elements in simple sentences. This practice focuses only on compound subjects and verbs, but you can expand the concept to compound objects.

J Answers, page 135:

1 Summer (s); is (v)
2 People (s); enjoy (v)
3 Fall (s1); spring (s2); seem (v)
4 leaves (s1); colors (s2); are (v)
5 trees (s1); plants (s2); get (v)
6 baseball (s1); soccer (s2); are (v)
7 friends (s); do ski (v1); skate (v2)
8 Skiing (s1); snowboarding (s2); are (v1); cause (v2)

2 1 At this university; students (s); in English classes; buy (v); from the bookstore
2 Before Friday; class (s); with a new teacher; must go (v); to the bookstore
3 book (s); with a map; on the cover; contains (v1); costs (v2); over $70
4 man (s1); woman (s2); next to my roommates; in the photos; taught (v); in Mexico
5 man (s1); with a boy; on his shoulders; comes (v); from Italy

K Compound sentences, page 136

Learning to combine simple sentences into compound sentences is an important step for students in making their writing more mature. Although there are other ways to form compound sentences, this book presents the seven coordinating conjunctions often referred to as the FANBOYS. All seven are presented in the box, but practice is provided with only *and, but,* and *so.*

K Answers, page 136:

1 people (s); want (v); cars (do); , but; others (s); want (v); cars (do)
2 people (s); have (v); tastes (do); , so; carmakers (s); manufacture (v); models (do)
3 customers (s); enjoy (v); driving (do); , and; dealers (s); encourage (v); drives (do)
4 economy (s1); handling (s2); are (v); , but; customers (s); like (v); styling (do)
5 buying (s1); is (v); , so; customers (s); bring (v); friends (do1); family (do2)

2 1 Racing bikes have narrow tires, but mountain bikes have wide tires (also *and*)
2 Mountain bikes travel off the trail, so they need wider, softer tires.
3 Wide tires provide softness, and narrow tires provide speed. (also *but*)

3 1 S
2 C
3 S
4 C
5 S

L Complex sentences, page 137

In addition to simple and compound sentences, complex sentences are the third type of sentence that students need to be able to recognize and form. Like compound sentences, complex sentences contain two clauses, but one of the clauses is a subordinate clause. Although there are many subordinate clause signals, only a few are used here. At the simplest, review the FANBOYS that are used to form compound sentences before focusing on the idea that subordinate clauses begin with signal words, but different ones. Write the words *when, if,* and *who* on the board, and ask students to name other similar words as a warm-up.

L Answers, page 137:

1 1 MC Flowers bloom in the spring.
2 SC
3 SC
4 MC Good spelling is important to a writer.
5 MC Hamsters make good pets.
6 SC
7 SC
8 MC It is hard to find a parking place.
9 SC
10 MC What did he eat?

2 1 Cookbooks are often bestsellers (MC); that have many color photographs (SC)
2 What readers enjoy are the color photographs. (MC); What readers enjoy (SC)
3 their cookbooks rarely sell well these days (MC); When publishers do not include color photographs (SC)
4 Readers like photographs (MC); because they show how the food looks (SC)
5 Everyone knows that beautiful cookbooks are expensive. (MC); that beautiful cookbooks are expensive (SC)
6 The cook is quite famous (MC); who wrote the new cookbook (SC)

3 1 S
2 C
3 CX
4 CX
5 C
6 CX
7 CX
8 S
9 C
10 CX

M Types of subordinate clauses, page 138

This is a brief presentation and practice of subordinate clauses. Only a few subordinating conjunctions are listed and used here. Most grammar books contain a fuller listing of these words.

M Answers, page 138:

1 1 After I finished (ADV)
2 What you wrote (N)
3 what you wrote (N)
4 who lost their folders (ADJ)
5 while Mary dances (ADV)
6 If Paul sings (ADV)
7 what Paul will sing (N)
8 if you will go (ADV)
9 when they can (ADV)
10 although she has a nice voice (ADV)

N Paragraphs and the position of topic sentences, pages 138–139

Although most paragraphs in this book have deductive or deductive-restatement organization, the reading materials that students encounter often contain examples of all types.

N Answers, page 139:

1 **1** b
2 c
3 d
4 a

O Capitalization, pages 139–140

This topic is complex, and only a few useful rules are presented here.

O Answers, page 140:

1 **1** My boyfriend and I love the movie called *Titanic.* (Italicize or underline the title.)
2 The book called *Harry Potter and the Sorcerer's Stone* was popular in 2001. (Italicize or underline the title.)
3 Elizabeth will take the TOEFL on Monday.
4 Mr. Smith's mother is living in the U.S.
5 Charles wants to get an M.A. degree or a Ph.D. degree at the University of Michigan.
6 After I talked to Professor Jones, I went to the library to study English.

P Punctuation marks and other symbols, pages 140–141

Students usually enjoy learning these names in English. Point out to students that titles of books, newspapers, magazines, and movies are usually underlined when written in handwriting and italicized when written on a computer.

P Answers, pages 140–141:

5 5 sentences

For Both Children and Adults

I read Harry Potter and the Sorcerer's Stone by J. K. Rowling recently. Have you read it? I was very surprised that I liked it so much. I knew it was a children's book, and I'm not a child anymore. I think Rowling is a good author because both adults and children enjoy her books.

2 **1** She loves to put strawberries, raspberries, or blueberries on her morning cereal.
2 Careful writers plan carefully, write several drafts, make many revisions, and do careful editing when they are writing important papers.
3 With no time, money, or energy left, she sat down on a park bench and cried.
4 It is easy to meet people in a dorm, at a coffee shop, or in a chat room.
5 There are no windows, tables, or other facilities in his small cell.

3 Have students suggest an appropriate title.

A Bad Day

How frustrating yesterday was! Why did I even get up? My bus was a half hour late. I spilled coffee on my new white shirt. My boss was in a terrible mood all day because her bus broke down on the way from home. In my apartment, there was water everywhere but no electricity. What a day!

4 Note that compound sentences are introduced on page 29 and practiced in item K on page 126.

1 Halloween is next week, so everyone needs a costume.
2 When people go to Halloween parties, they wear costumes.
3 Some costumes are expensive, but many wonderful ones are not.
4 Because people want to make jack-o-lanterns, they buy pumpkins.
5 After you carve a pumpkin, you put a candle inside.
6 People in the United States gather with their families when it is time for Thanksgiving dinner.
7 The adults enjoy talking, and the children like to play.
8 Although turkey is the most popular food on Thanksgiving, some families prefer beef or pork.
9 Some people watch a football game after dinner.
10 Turkeys are very big, so many people have turkey sandwiches the day after Thanksgiving.

5

Joe walked into the plane before the flight attendant closed the door. He walked out when the plane landed. Where was Joe? He was in Toronto.

Joe walked into the plane. Before the flight attendant closed the door, he walked out. When the plane landed, where was Joe? He was still in Chicago.

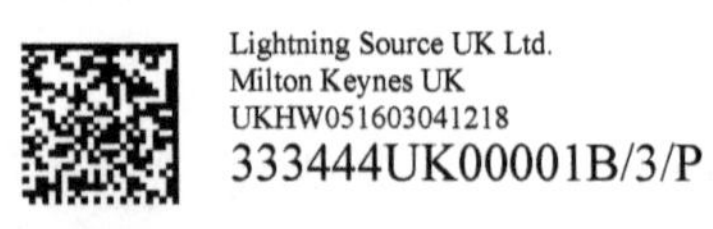
Lightning Source UK Ltd.
Milton Keynes UK
UKHW051603041218
333444UK00001B/3/P

9 780521 671361